I
HATE
OKLAHOMA

PETE DAVIS

TRIUMPH
BOOKS

CONTENTS

INTRODUCTION

IN 1859 THE BROTHER OF Chief John Ross of the Cherokee tribe was drilling for salt water near Salina on the Grand River in the Territory of Oklahoma. Now most people would drill for oil, or natural gas, or even fresh water, but this being Oklahoma, he felt the need for salt water. Maybe he wanted to make taffy.

This Jed Clampett of the Okies struck black gold, and the history of Oklahoma was changed forever. But for every good deed there must be some punishment, and that punishment appeared 36 years later when the University of Oklahoma fielded their first football team.

I Hate Oklahoma is here to show you some things you may not yet know about the clodhopping team you love to hate. You may think you know the history, but this book will take a new and fresh look at the embarrassing first 117 years of Oklahoma football—and get you ready for the next 117—by digging up some amazing information you haven't seen or heard before.

Here are just some of the nuggets of fascinating history surrounding this lamest of football programs, information that every college football fan should know by heart, or soon will when they read this book:

★ An opponent once tried to use a kitchen appliance as a weapon during a game against Oklahoma. They were justified.

★ An OU player had to swim a frozen creek to score a touchdown.

★ Oklahoma is the only major college team to have four different head coaches win 100 games apiece. Yet they still manage to suck mule ass.

★ An OU head coach left the job to prospect for gold in the Arctic. Another left to return to medical school. The stated goal of most Oklahoma graduates is to leave the state. You can even major in leaving at OU.

★ Oklahoma once hired a head coach just to teach the team a trick play. He then left.

★ A man named Biff was once head coach. Also a man named Snorter and another named Gomer. Not too surprising, actually.

★ A Sooner became a Hollywood movie star, and surprisingly not in the porn industry.

★ One of the school fight songs was written for a cigarette.

These are just a few of the scintillating Sooners facts you'll discover in *I Hate Oklahoma*. This book will also renew your faith in incompetence and give you tons of trivia to use against those hated Sooners fans or to win a few adult beverages from your friends and family.

Many a young boy grew up watching the Red River Shootout between Texas and Oklahoma and spent their afternoons pretending to be an option quarterback for Oklahoma and dishing out spectacular, last-second feeds to imaginary tailbacks. They made themselves learn to pitch the football accurately with both right and left hands. They then realized to achieve their goal they would actually have to live *in* Oklahoma, and they quickly abandoned the silly idea.

Many a Sooners fan grew up wanting to don the red and white uniform and race out onto Owen Field. They also grew up wanting clothes that fit and something other than raw turnips for supper, but that didn't happen either.

Boomer Sooner! (Which is Native American for "offensive holding.")

1
WE HATE LOSING TO THE SOONERS

SOONERS FANS COME IN ALL shapes, sizes, ages, creeds, religions, genders, and waist sizes. And we hate them all. While the majority live, play, and work in the state of Oklahoma, there are thousands of them sprinkled around the globe spreading Sooner Sickness. The annual Red River Shootout is held in Dallas, which is almost dead center between the two schools, being about 197 miles from Austin and 190 from Norman.

The Longhorns have a whopping big edge in the series, but unfortunately, through pure luck or food poisoning, OU has managed to pull out some victories over the years. Here are some of the more forgettable losses to this blight from that dust tundra to the north. All of these losses will be wiped from memory when the time machine they're working on at UT finally becomes fully operational.

October 14, 1950

OKLAHOMA	7	0	0	7	14
TEXAS	0	7	0	6	13

Fourth-ranked Texas was up by six points with just four minutes left before third-ranked Oklahoma recovered a fumble

OU DEFENSIVE RECORDS vs. TEXAS

* The most tackles ever recorded in a game against Texas by a Sooner came in 1974 when senior linebacker Rod Shoate had 21 tackles. Second-ranked OU squeaked out a 16–13 victory over 17th-ranked UT that day. The All-American Shoate dominated the game despite suffering an arm injury in the first half. Besides his 21 tackles, Shoate recovered a fumble and broke up two passes.

* The second-most tackles by a Sooner against Texas came in 2008, when sophomore linebacker Travis Lewis brought down 19 Longhorns, but No. 5 UT still upset top-ranked OU that day, 45–35.

and beat UT 14–13. This game was the coming out party for the Sooners' Billy Vessels. The sophomore halfback scored two touchdowns, including the go-ahead score with a few minutes to play after the Longhorns fumbled a punt attempt deep in their own territory. It was the only game the Horns would lose that season.

OU head coach Bud Wilkinson said, "It took a fumbled punt to beat Texas."

What was even more galling was that if the Longhorns could have just held on for the victory, the Sooners probably wouldn't have gone on to win their first national championship that season, the first of three under Wilkinson. That deserves a *dagnammit.*

October 10, 1953

OKLAHOMA	6	6	0	7	19
TEXAS	0	0	0	14	14

It was bad enough that No. 15 Texas was upset by No. 16 Oklahoma 19–14, but it was even worse that it began a record-setting 47-game winning streak for OU. Oklahoma didn't lose again until November 1957, when they were shut out at home by Notre Dame—which is possibly the only other team with fans that could rival the Sooners for obnoxiousness and body odor.

The Sooners passed for only 13 yards on a day when the temperature in Dallas hit 91 degrees. It's not surprising that Oklahoma played so well in the heat. They had already had to learn how, since air conditioning didn't appear in that state until 1992.

October 8, 1955

OKLAHOMA	6	7	7	0	20
TEXAS	0	0	0	0	0

The third-ranked Oklahoma inbreds celebrated the 50th meeting of the Red River Shootout with a 20–0 win over the unranked Longhorns. They intercepted the Horns five times, with linebacker Jerry Tubbs making the pick three times; Tubbs also played center on offense. It was the first time OU had shut out Texas in 17 years, the seventh time overall. The Sooners would go on to win their second national title that season. It hurts to even type that sentence.

October 13, 1956

OKLAHOMA	6	13	13	13	**45**
TEXAS	0	0	0	0	**0**

UT was the last in a trio of consecutive shutouts by No. 1 Oklahoma as OU embarrassed Texas 45–0. Clendon Thomas and Tommy McDonald each had three touchdowns as the Sooners went on to win their third national championship, the second in a row. Oklahoma would shut out six teams that season and outscore their opponents 466–51.

It was the fifth year in a row that the Sooners had won the rivalry game. But leave it to OU to belong to a stupid conference that didn't allow their schools to go to bowl games in two consecutive years! What was possibly the best Sooners team of all time had to sit home on their dust farms on New Year's Day and watch other teams play. That's if the clodhoppers could get the town's television to work.

October 12, 1974

OKLAHOMA	0	7	0	9	**16**
TEXAS	0	3	7	3	**13**

This game brought to mind shades of 1950 as 17th-ranked Texas led 13–7 in the fourth quarter over top-ranked OU. Split end Billy Brooks raced a reverse 40 yards for the game-tying score. The score stood at 13–13 after a missed extra point until linebacker Rod Shoate recovered a fumble at mid-field. Tony DiRienzo hit a 37-yard field goal for the 16–13 win. Shoate also had 21 tackles and a forced fumble in the game.

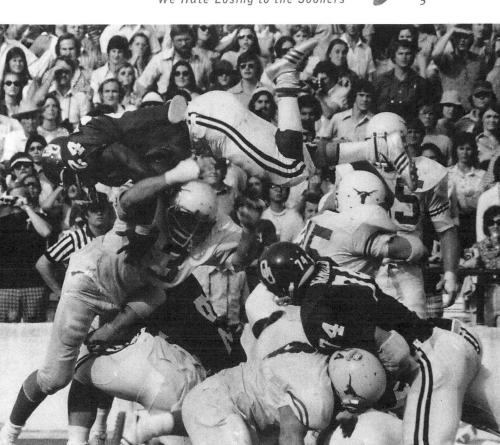

Oklahoma running back Joe Washington (24) leaps high for a first down against Texas in the fourth quarter of the Sooners' 16–13 win in 1974. The Longhorns' Bill Hamilton (13) makes the stop.

Oklahoma would go on to win their fourth national title that year, the first of three under head coach and bootlegger's boy Barry Switzer, who led the team known as "The Best Team Money Can Buy."

October 11, 1975

OKLAHOMA	10	0	7	7	**24**
TEXAS	0	7	0	10	**17**

This year's Red River Rivalry featured the fast feet of Joe Washington for No. 2 Oklahoma against the pounding running style of fifth-ranked UT's Earl Campbell. Yet it was Horace Ivory who stole the spotlight with his 33-yard run for the winning touchdown in a 24–17 victory for OU.

OU RUSHING RECORDS vs. TEXAS

* In 1997 running back De'Mond Parker rushed for the most yards ever by a Sooner against UT with 291 yards in 31 rushing attempts. The sophomore also scored three touchdowns during that game, but the Longhorns got the last laugh with a 27–24 victory. It was the first time in nearly three decades that neither team was ranked coming into the contest, and it was the first time ever that both teams had a losing record. Parker out-dueled junior running back Ricky Williams, who rushed for 223 yards and two scores. Parker fell just three yards short of the all-time OU rushing record set by Greg Pruitt. It was Pruitt's old rushing record against Texas that Parker eclipsed in this game. After the game, Parker said the loss was like a dagger through his heart and that he would have traded all his yards for a win.

* The second-most yards by a Sooners running back against UT came in 2002, when Quentin Griffin rushed for 248 yards, which puts him in a tie with Steve Owens for the ninth-most yards ever amassed by an OU back in a single game.

The Longhorns were led at quarterback by senior Marty Akins, who was the first QB to start three straight seasons under head coach Darrell Royal. But the Sooners may have had the Lord on their side, as their signal-caller was ordained minister Steve Davis.

The Sooners went on after this game to win their fifth national championship, their second in a row. It was the second time in their history that they won the championship two years in a row. Just makes you wanna puke.

Many Oklahoma players lamented having to enter the NFL draft, as they were not looking forward to the pay cut they would be taking when they left Norman.

October 12, 1985

OKLAHOMA	0	7	0	7	14
TEXAS	7	0	0	0	7

The high-powered offense of No. 2–ranked Oklahoma could only score 14 points against 17th-ranked Texas, but it was enough, as the defense put together one of their greatest games ever by holding UT to just four first downs and negative yardage in the second half for a 14–7 win.

They did it without nose guard Tony Casillas, who left early in the game with a knee injury. Linebacker Brian Bosworth came up big with an interception and was named the Big 8 Defensive Player of the Week. But it's still funny to see the highlight film of that blowhard Bosworth being bulldozed by Bo Jackson when they were both in the NFL.

Coach Switzer called it the greatest defensive performance by the Sooners in the 20 years he'd been associated with the program. Pardon me, Coach Switzer, please pick up the white courtesy phone—it's a call from the NCAA Infractions Committee.

Yes, OU went on to win their sixth national title. This never gets any easier to type. I know it's hard for you to read, too. We'll get through this together.

October 7, 2000

OKLAHOMA	14	28	14	7	63
TEXAS	0	7	0	7	14

Hopefully this is the last time I ever have to mention Oklahoma and the national championship in the same sentence. "Red October" is what OU fans now call this month in a play on words based on the movie title *The Hunt for Red October*. Hey, I never said these Sooners were known for their originality. No. 11 Texas fell 63–14 to a 10th-ranked Sooners team.

This embarrassing score was the worst loss for UT in the history of the rivalry. It was also the first signature win for Bob Stoops as head coach. Oklahoma was led by running back Quentin Griffin with a team single-game record of six touchdowns.

It was the eighth-straight meeting between the two rivals in which the Longhorns could not score in the first quarter. Both starting quarterback Major Applewhite and backup Chris Simms

Oklahoma's Curtis Fagan (12) scampers eight yards for a touchdown against Texas during the second quarter of the Sooners' 63–14 dismantling of the Longhorns on October 7, 2000.

were ineffective. OU's Josh Heupel was like a surgeon operating on the UT defense. Texas head coach Mack Brown said, "It wasn't even a game, because we did not play in the first half."

The second half was no picnic either.

November 8, 2003

OKLAHOMA	14	23	14	14	**65**
TEXAS	7	6	0	0	**13**

Remember when I mentioned earlier that Texas lost to Oklahoma 63–14 in 2000? Well, if that was hard to take, you might not want to read the rest of this breakdown of the 2003 game.

The 65–13 win by No. 1 Oklahoma is the largest margin ever for an OU victory over UT, which came into the game ranked No. 11. Longhorns quarterback Vince Young passed for 135 yards and ran for 127 in relief of starter Chance Mock, who had come down with a bug—the interception bug—early

OU PASSING RECORDS vs. TEXAS

* The most a Sooners quarterback has ever passed for yardage against UT in a single game came in 2008, when sophomore Sam Bradford threw for 387 yards on 28 completions. It's the 20th-most yards ever passed for in one game by an Oklahoma QB. Bradford threw five touchdowns but also two interceptions, as fifth-ranked Texas went on to upend No. 1 OU 45–35. Those five TD passes are also the most ever by a Sooners quarterback against Texas.

* The second-most passing yards amassed in one game by a Sooner against UT came in 2011, when Landry Jones threw for 367 yards on 31 completions in a game won by OU 55–17.

* The second-most touchdown passes for a Sooners QB against UT came in 2003, when senior Jason White threw four of them in a 65–13 win for Oklahoma.

in the game. But it wasn't enough to stop the Crimson and Cream floodwaters.

This is not a game for dissecting or rehashing. To steal a line from Monty Python, this is a game for lying down and avoiding.

October 9, 2004

OKLAHOMA	0	3	3	6	**12**
TEXAS	0	0	0	0	**0**

At least No. 2 Oklahoma didn't score over 60 points in this win over No. 5 Texas. Unfortunately, UT didn't score *any* points, and was shut out 12–0.

Freshman OU running back Adrian Peterson ran for 225 yards as the Sooners won this rivalry game for the fifth consecutive season. It was the first time in 282 games that the Longhorns had been blanked, the longest such streak in the country at that time.

At least the Texas defense showed up. Oklahoma didn't score their touchdown until there were only eight minutes left in the contest.

Senior Longhorns running back Cedric Benson was held to just 92 yards rushing, which was well below his NCAA-leading average of 187 per game. Almost 80,000 fans attended, which was the most ever in the nearly 100 years of the rivalry. Too bad the UT offense didn't attend.

OU RECEIVING RECORDS vs. TEXAS

★ The most yards receiving by an Oklahoma player against Texas was in 2003, when junior wide receiver Mark Clayton caught eight passes for 190 yards and one touchdown and helped the top-ranked Sooners win the game 65–13. At the time, it set the all-time OU record for single-game receiving yards, but it has since been surpassed four times, including twice by Ryan Broyles. Broyles now holds the all-time Oklahoma single-game receiving yards record at 217 in a game against Kansas in 2011.

★ The second-most receiving yards by a Sooner in a game against UT came in 1992, when junior Corey Warren caught nine passes for 187 yards and a touchdown, but the Longhorns won the game 34–24.

2

WE LOVE TO HATE
OKLAHOMA PLAYERS

DARRELL ROYAL

DARRELL ROYAL. *Darrell Royal?!*

Yes, *that* Darrell Royal. Believe it or not, he began his college football career on the wrong side of the tracks as an Oklahoma Sooner. And during his tenure in Norman, he was an OU player worth hating.

Royal played both quarterback and defensive back, and he could also punt as well as anyone. He left Oklahoma as the all-time school record-holder for interceptions, with 17. He also had punt returns for touchdowns of 73 and 95 yards. In fact, there was little he could not do on a football field.

During his All-America senior year of 1949, he only threw one interception. But that's not as amazing as it sounds, since he only threw 63 passes all season.

The Sooners were 36–6–1 during Royal's four seasons, but it's only fitting that he was only 2–2 against Texas.

After being drafted by the New York Bulldogs in 1950, Royal would go on to become the greatest head coach in Longhorns history—and a major pain in the side for his alma mater. Before coming to Austin, he first served as head coach of the Edmonton Eskimos of the Canadian Football League. From there he headed to a much warmer but still godforsaken outpost in Starkville, where he was head coach at Mississippi State, and later worked at the University of Washington before heading to his proper destiny in Austin.

Talk about a love/hate relationship! But he redeemed his sins by coming over from the dark side.

BRIAN BOSWORTH

Where does one start with the story of Brian Bosworth? Why not start with the letter A—for *A-hole*.

The "Boz" thought of himself as a star both on and off the field, and his fans agreed. He's the only player to ever win the Dick Butkus Award twice for being the best linebacker in the country. Amazingly, this All-American in 1985 and 1986 was also an Academic All-American. A Sooner! Yes, it surprised everyone, and a recount was immediately launched.

The Boz was drafted by the Seahawks, receiving the largest rookie contract in NFL history at the time, $11 million for 10 years—of which he earned about $10.14. Prior to the supplemental draft, Bosworth sent letters to many NFL teams stating that he would not play for them, so they needn't bother to even try to draft him. A pro soccer team actually chose him in

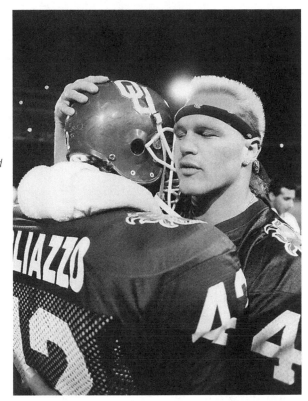

Sooners linebacker Brian Bosworth hugs a teammate before kickoff of the 1987 Orange Bowl against Arkansas. The "Boz" was barred from playing because it was discovered he had been using steriods. Oops.

their draft because they said they had never received a letter instructing them not to!

Bosworth mocked Denver quarterback John Elway to the point that thousands of Broncos fans wore "Ban the Boz" T-shirts. Unknown to them, Bosworth's T-shirt company made the shirts. He wasn't Academic All-American for nothing.

Boz is famously remembered, to the everlasting laughter of Longhorns fans, for the colossal goal-line collision between himself and Raiders running legend Bo Jackson. Let's just say Jackson got the better of Boz. The Boz had bragged that he would contain Jackson, but instead this impressive Raider rushed for over 200 yards and scored three touchdowns, earning one of them by running roughshod over Bosworth.

The Boz is now an actor in Hollywood known mostly for action flicks in which he beats up characters more annoying than he is...when they can be found.

LANDRY JONES

Sophomore quarterback Landry Jones won the 2010 Sammy Baugh Trophy for being the nation's best passer. It's presented annually by the Touchdown Club of Columbus, Ohio, and has been around since 1959.

There must be a lot of drinking during voting.

Jones threw a school-record six touchdown passes as a freshman filling in for injured china doll Sam Bradford. But there should be an asterisk next to this record, as Jones achieved it against Tulsa, a team that looks at defense like it looks at culture—as something to avoid at all costs.

Jones is 2–1 in his three games against the Longhorns, and has thrown six touchdowns and two interceptions. But he took a No. 1–ranked team at the start of the 2011 season and ended up in the not-so-prestigious Insight Bowl against a 7–5 Iowa Hawkeyes team, a game in which Oklahoma coach Bob Stoops got to face his alma mater. I know, I know—Stoops went to college?! You can't spell *stoopid* without *Stoop*. Despite this handicap, OU managed to win 31–14.

Landry Jones, sucker for punishment that he is, is returning for his senior season.

BILLY VESSELS

Billy Vessels exploded onto the scene during the 1950 season and saved a special game just for Texas. The sophomore halfback crossed the goal line twice that game, once for the go-ahead score with a few minutes to play, leading the Sooners to a 14–13 come-from-behind victory. It was the only game UT would lose that season, and Oklahoma would go on to beat Nebraska for the national title.

Vessels—or should we call him by his nickname, "Curly"?— was the first OU player to win the Heisman Trophy, after his 1952 senior season. (No word on how Moe and Larry took the news.)

Curly scored 17 touchdowns that year and rushed for over 1,000 yards. He even threw for two scores. During his four years in Norman, he only lost to the Longhorns once.

But Curly wasn't good enough for the NFL, so he froze his toes off in the Canadian Football League for the Edmonton Eskimos. I would tell you how he won the prestigious Schenley Award as the best pro player in Canada, except no one south of Manitoba has ever heard of it and therefore you could care less.

Vessels made up for wearing the Sooners uniform by later wearing the uniform of an officer in the United States Army.

He was elected to the National Football Foundation and College Hall of Fame in 1974.

STEVE OWENS

Tailback Steve Owens became the second Sooner to win the Heisman in 1969. He not only owned several OU records, he left school with NCAA records, too. Owens' 4,041 yards rushing was the most ever in the nation at the time, and he held the mark for most net yards rushing in one season, 1,649 in 1968.

Owens' 57 touchdowns is an Oklahoma record; he also holds the record for most TDs in a season, with 23, and most points in a season, with 138. He once ran for over 100 yards in 17 straight games, an NCAA record at the time, and received the Walter Camp Trophy for his achievements. But for all his glory, he was 0–3 against Texas.

Owens was the 19th pick overall by the Detroit Lions in 1970. He entered the National Football Foundation Hall of Fame in 1991 and was the director of athletics at the University of Oklahoma from 1996 to 1998. (In other words, he was responsible for all of their balls.)

Owens has also been a broadcaster for Sooners games. So, like Landry Jones, he's also a sucker for punishment. Owens enjoys his work despite the fact that most Oklahomans having trouble understanding him (since he broadcasts the games in English).

BILLY SIMS

The 1978 Heisman went to running back Billy Sims, who became the third Sooner to win it. Sims had more than 500 carries and set the NCAA record for average yards per rush with an astounding seven yards per rush. (Sounds a little greedy to me.) Sims led the country in scoring in both 1978 and 1979, and was a two-time All-American. He won the Davey O'Brien Award in 1978.

What makes Sims' success worse is that he's a native Texan! Barry Switzer kept an assistant parked in Sims' hometown, Hooks, for almost three months in order to woo him to Norman. During his five seasons at Oklahoma, his teams went 2–2–1 against UT. (Sims did sit out one of those seasons due to an injury.)

Sims was the first player chosen in the 1980 draft by the Lions, and was having a great NFL career before a knee injury ended it prematurely. In 1995 he became the 11th Sooner to enter the National Football Foundation Hall of Fame.

Sims has opened several barbeque restaurants in Oklahoma, which seems to be the 401k retirement plan for most OU players. You can purchase "Billy bucks"—printed-up fake money—to use at his establishments. Sounds like something Coach Switzer would be involved in.

SAM BRADFORD

Quarterback Sam Bradford became the fifth Sooner to win the Heisman Trophy in 2008. He then rang the bell at the New York Stock Exchange, and the Dow went up 100 points

Oklahoma's future Heisman Trophy–winning QB, Sam Bradford, passes against Texas in the third quarter of their 2007 meeting, which the Sooners won 28–21, in no small part thanks to Bradford's three touchdown passes.

that day. (The traders were just happy that Bradford wasn't on the football field.)

He won the Davey O'Brien Award and the Sammy Baugh Trophy, and was named the Big 12 Offensive Player of the Year and National Player of the Year by both CBSsports.com and the *Sporting News*. (Show-off.)

Bradford led the first offense to score over 700 points in a season since the modern era of college football began around

World War II, scoring 716 points when all was said and done. His OU team also became the first to score 60 points or more in five straight games in this era.

Bradford led the nation with 50 touchdown passes, and also led his team to a third consecutive Big 12 championship and a spot in the national championship game, which they lost—again. That's such an endearing habit they've picked up recently. It almost makes them cute. (I said almost.)

In 2007 Bradford set the NCAA freshman record with 36 touchdown passes. At the tender age of 19, he led Oklahoma to a 28–21 win over UT by throwing three touchdowns. In 2008 he threw five touchdowns for the No. 1 Sooners against Texas, but two of his passes were completed to Longhorns, which helped No. 5 UT pull off an upset victory, 45–35.

In 2009 Aaron Williams showed little respect for the Heisman winner when he knocked the stink off of Bradford with a sack that put him out of the game in the first quarter. For all of his talent, Bradford's right arm sometimes seemed attached to his shoulder with silly string. That injury put him out for the rest of the season and ended his college career.

Bradford was also an Academic All-American, so that arm injury must not have stopped him from taking tests. (Oh, who am I kidding—this is OU! They have people for that.)

DERRICK STRAIT

The Nagurski Trophy is named for former Golden Gophers and NFL great Bronko Nagurski, one of the toughest men to ever play the game. Derrick Strait won the award in 2003. UT fans hate Strait for one game in particular. During this 65–13 destruction of the Longhorns in 2003, he single-handedly recovered two fumbles, intercepted a pass, deflected three others, and had 11 tackles. He also emceed the coin flip and painted the end zones.

Derrick set school records for passes broken up (53), career interception return yards (397), and starts (53), and was an All-America defensive back in 2003. Texas fans do not miss seeing him on Saturdays.

JERRY TUBBS

In 1955 Oklahoma linebacker Jerry Tubbs became the hero of the Red River Shootout by intercepting three passes in the Sooners win. Tubbs was an even better offensive center, and was named an All-American at that position. He even played a little at fullback.

OU never lost to Texas during the three seasons Tubbs played varsity football. In fact, he never lost to anyone, going undefeated from 1954 to 1956. Tubbs was even an Academic All-American, which gave him more of an IQ than most towns in Oklahoma.

After escaping Norman, Tubbs played 10 years in the NFL for the Chicago Cardinals, the San Francisco 49ers, and the Dallas Cowboys. After retiring, he worked as an assistant coach in Dallas for 21 seasons. Tubbs was inducted into the College Football Hall of Fame in 1996.

CLAUDE REEDS

Claude Reeds was the first Sooner to be named an All-American, way back in 1913. He was a fullback at a time when fullbacks also threw the ball. He was also a tight end and a punter; in fact, in 1911 he punted a ball 102 yards in a kick against Texas.

Reeds was so good that in 1913, Missouri refused to play Oklahoma if he was on the team. So the OU squad voted to play without him—and lost to Mizzou by three points. Serves them right for backstabbing their teammate and best player.

Reeds won three out of the four games in which he played against UT. He was inducted into the National Football Foundation College Football Hall of Fame in 1961.

JASON WHITE

In 2003 quarterback Jason White became the fourth Sooner, and the first at his position, to win the Heisman Trophy. He was also named Player of the Year by the *Sporting News*, CNNSI.com, and the Associated Press. He overcame not one, but two season-ending injuries during his six-year college career. (But hey, at least he graduated faster than the average Oklahoma student.) He set an OU record with 40 touchdown passes while also taking home the Davey O'Brien Award and Big 12 Offensive Player of the Year honors. White won the O'Brien in 2003 and 2004, and was also named the Player of the Year by the *Sporting News* and *Sports Illustrated*.

White was 17 of 21 in one 65–14 spanking of UT, which made his glamour shot popular on dartboards throughout the pubs of Austin.

You'd think with all these collegiate accolades, White would have become a star in the NFL too. Think again. Even Joe Namath thought White's knees were sketchy. He retired after his knees took one look at an NFL pass rush and buckled.

JOSH HEUPEL

Josh Heupel came in second in the Heisman voting in 2000 despite being named the Player of the Year by CBS and the Associated Press, as well as winning the Walter Camp Trophy. After leading the Sooners to the national championship that season, he became the first OU quarterback to be named an All-American in 29 years, and the first to be consensus All-American. Heupel threw for 53 touchdowns in just two seasons as the starter. He was 1–1 against UT.

Not content with being a pain in the arse to Texas as just a player, Heupel returned to coach at Oklahoma, where he is now the co-offensive coordinator, QB coach, and Chief Pillow Fluffer.

Heupel has the bizarre distinction of being the losing quarterback in both the last OU game played in the 20th century and the first played in the 21st. The 1999 Independence Bowl in Shreveport, Louisiana, began the night of December 31, 1999. But it ended just after midnight on January 1, 2000, when Ole Miss kicked a field goal as time expired for a 27–25 win over

Heupel and OU. It was the last time he and the Sooners would lose until October of 2001.

QUENTIN GRIFFIN

Running back Quentin Griffin had the game of his life on October 7, 2000. Unfortunately, it came against the Longhorns. Griffin set a school record and tied the Big 12 Conference mark with six rushing touchdowns in the 63–14 victory over Texas. As a senior in 2002, he rushed for 248 yards and a TD, and caught another in Oklahoma's 35–24 win over UT.

He also scored the only TD in the national championship game win over Florida State on January 3, 2001. Griffin can just go away now.

ADRIAN PETERSON

Adrian Peterson was the first freshman in 2004 to become a finalist for the Doak Walker Legends Award. He rushed for 15 touchdowns and 1,925 yards that season, and led the nation with 339 rushing attempts. He was also invited to the Heisman Trophy ceremony along with teammate and 2003 winner Jason White. He broke three NCAA records for freshman backs, including most rushing attempts, most 100-yard rushing games (with 11), and most consecutive 100-yard rushing games (with nine). But it was his performance against Texas that was the most offensive.

On October 9, 2004, Peterson ran for 225 yards in a 12–0 win over the No. 5 Longhorns. Despite rushing for over 1,000

Oklahoma's Adrian Peterson gets chased down by Texas' Brian Robison during the Sooners' 12–0 win in 2004. Peterson racked up 225 yards rushing on the day against the then–No. 5 Longhorns. Photo courtesy of Getty Images

yards in each of his three seasons in Norman, he was only 1–2 against UT.

Peterson has become a star in the NFL after being drafted by the Vikings—that is, when he doesn't have a hangnail or a head cold that keeps him out of the lineup. He's about as reliable as an OU diploma.

KEITH JACKSON

Tight end Keith Jackson was the first Sooner to receive an NCAA Top Six Award, which is given annually to the top six athletes in the country no matter what sport they play—even if they do hail from Oklahoma. He was an All-American tight end in 1986 and 1987. While a junior, he averaged nearly 29 yards per catch; this stat was even more amazing given the fact that the Sooners didn't pass much that season. (Back then, OU looked at passing like prairie dogs look at hawks.)

Jackson could catch, block, and run—none of which is required to graduate from OU. Drafted by the Eagles, he won a Super Bowl with the Packers and later worked in the broadcast booth for NFL games and for the Oklahoma Sooner Football Radio Network. In December 2001 Jackson became the 15th Oklahoma player to be inducted into the College Football Hall of Fame.

GREG PRUITT

Halfback Greg Pruitt was an incredibly gifted player who had the misfortune of playing at the same time as another all-time great, the Huskers' Johnny Rodgers, who beat Pruitt out of the Heisman in 1972. (Longhorns fans call this justice.)

Pruitt was the NCAA Football Player of the Year during that same season. He set the NCAA record with 9.4 yards per carry, and was an All-American halfback in 1971 and 1972. He earned the school record for most yards in a game when he amassed 294 against Kansas State in 1971. Big deal—Betty White could have gained 100 yards on K-State in those days. (And she would have, too, if not for twisting an ankle in the third quarter of one game.) Pruitt was drafted by the Browns in 1973 and was inducted into the National Football Foundation College Football Hall of Fame in 1999.

JOE WASHINGTON

The NCAA Football Player of the Year award is given out annually by the Pigskin Club of Washington, D.C. Halfback Joe Washington, one of the most electrifying players in Sooners history, took the award home in 1974.

Washington was another Texas boy gone wrong, having left Port Arthur for the dusty streets of Norman. He was so enamored with Coach Barry Switzer that he even volunteered to baby-sit for his kids. He replaced Greg Pruitt as the team's main offensive weapon—which is fitting, since Pruitt recruited him. Washington never lost to UT during his four seasons.

Some consider his signature game to be one of those played during OU's march to a second straight national title in 1975.

Late in the fourth quarter, OU was losing by seven to Missouri when Washington suddenly broke off a 70-yard dash for a touchdown. In those days there was no overtime, and OU could not afford a tie, so they went for the two-point conversion. "Little Joe" came through again, scoring the two points for the victory.

Washington's 5,781 all-purpose yards is still a Sooners record. He won two national titles during his four years while only twice feeling the sting of a loss. He finished his career as Oklahoma's all-time leading rusher.

Washington was taken fourth overall in the 1976 draft by the Chargers, but spent most of his NFL career in Washington, D.C. Joe is now the special assistant to the director of athletics at Oklahoma, and is married to Meadow Lark.

DARYL HUNT

Linebacker Daryl Hunt was a two-time All-American and a large, painful thorn in the side of all Longhorns. He was the first black football player for legendary high school program Odessa Permian, and would later come back to haunt his native state on the college gridiron. Hunt registered 18 tackles, an interception, and a sack in just one game against Texas. He set the Sooners record for tackles in a career, with 506.

Hunt was an All-American twice, in 1977 and 1978. He was drafted by the Houston Oilers in 1979 and played there for six years. Sadly, he passed away after suffering a heart attack in 2010.

THE SELMON BROTHERS

During the 1970s, the Sooners had probably the two best defensive linemen in college football playing for them at the same time—and they were brothers. Nose guard Dewey Selmon was one of them. On two national championship teams, in 1974 and 1975, Selmon was second in tackles only to his brother, Lee Roy, who won the Outland Trophy and the Lombardi Award.

The Selmons took their brother act to the NFL when both were drafted by the Buccaneers, Lee Roy in the first round and Dewey in the second. In fact, Lee Roy was the first player ever chosen by Tampa Bay, and Dewey was the second; the team later retired Lee Roy's number. The state of Florida even named a highway after Lee Roy. (When Texas fans told him to hit the road, he had his own road to hit!) In 1988 Lee Roy was elected into the College Football Hall of Fame; he later became the first Oklahoma player to be elected to the NFL Hall of Fame.

But it turns out that this fearsome twosome might never have played for OU if things had turned out a little differently. They were just hours away from signing with Colorado when a third brother, Lucious, was scouted by an assistant coach from Oklahoma who saw that all three brothers could play. Lucious was actually an All-American in 1973.

These brothers are now known for their barbecue sauce, which they serve at their restaurant in Wichita, Kansas. You can't swing a dead cat without hitting a barbecue joint run by an ex-Sooner.

Sibling defensive linemen Lee Roy (center) and Dewey Selmon (right) talk with Oklahoma head coach Barry Switzer a few days before the 1975 Orange Bowl in Miami against the No. 5 Michigan Wolverines. The Sooners won the game 14–6, along with their second straight national championship.

Their college coach and evil overlord, Barry Switzer, has called for a statue of the Selmon Brothers to be placed on the Oklahoma campus. He also called Lee Roy the greatest player he ever coached at Norman. Lee Roy Selmon passed away in September of 2011 after suffering a stroke. He was just 56.

DERLAND MOORE

Defensive tackle Derland Moore was an All-America defensive tackle and an all-American pain against UT in 1972. In the game against the Longhorns, he fell on a fumble in the end zone for a touchdown. Moore also blocked a punt that was recovered for a score in this 27–0 win, which earned him National Lineman of the Week honors.

But the football gods frowned on him in the NFL after he had the misfortune of being drafted by the horrible Saints. Calling himself "the Losingest Player in the NFL," Moore played in New Orleans for 13 seasons, never once making the playoffs. It wasn't until his 14th year in the league that he got to play in the postseason, and that was with the Jets. Hey, karma is a bitch.

JIM OWENS

End Jim Owens was a Texas nemesis. For you OU grads, the word *nemesis* means "pain in the ass." He caught a touchdown pass against them as a freshman, then caught the winning TD from quarterback Darrell Royal—yes, *that* Darrell Royal—as a senior.

Owens was an All-American in 1949. He was drafted by the Pittsburgh Steelers that same year, and was inducted into the National Football Foundation College Football Hall of Fame in 1982. Owens was also head coach of the Washington Huskies from 1957 to 1974, taking his team to victory in the Rose Bowl twice.

REGGIE KINLAW

Nose guard Reggie Kinlaw had a game against the Longhorns in 1978 that UT would like to forget. He caused a fumble, had 10 unassisted tackles, and assisted on five more in a 31–10 Oklahoma win. Kinlaw was an All-American in 1977 and 1978 and was drafted by the Oakland Raiders in 1979. He is currently a high school football coach in California—and hopefully has no plans to ever return to Texas.

JIMBO ELROD

All-America defensive end Jimbo Elrod set a school record with 44 tackles for a loss in 1975. He hit Earl Campbell so hard during a game against Texas that the running back fumbled, leading to a game-winning field goal for the Sooners. Elrod was drafted by the Chiefs in 1976 and also played for the Houston Oilers.

BILLY BROOKS

Split end Billy Brooks had a game-winning touchdown against the Longhorns. He only tasted defeat once during his time in Norman, while helping the Sooners to 32 wins and one tie. Brooks was an All-American in 1975. He was drafted in the first round by Cincinnati, and also played for the Oilers and the Chargers.

TONY CASILLAS

Nose guard Tony Casillas won the Vince Lombardi Award as the best lineman in the country. He was the UPI National

Lineman of the Year in 1984, as well as the Big 8 Defensive Player of the Year, and was a two-time All-American. He was 2–1–1 against UT.

Casillas was drafted in 1986 by the Falcons and played well for a while, but then spent most of his time in Atlanta pouting and whining and acting like he didn't even want to play football anymore. He was traded to Dallas, where he got his head on straight again. Even an Oklahoma player can find a better life in Texas.

SOONERS EVEN A LONGHORN CAN'T HATE

Bob Kalsu

James Robert "Bob" Kalsu was much more than just a Sooners football player.

He was an American Hero.

Kalsu was an offensive tackle and All-American in 1967. He was also in the ROTC program during the turbulent Vietnam War era. He was drafted by the Buffalo Bills in 1968 and played one year before being called to join the 101st Airborne Division of the U.S. Army. Kalsu refused any special treatment, saying he made a promise to his country, and just because he played football, that didn't make him any more special than any other soldier.

He was stationed at Firebase Ripcord in South Vietnam when, on July 21, 1970, he was killed by North Vietnamese mortar fire, becoming the only professional football player to be killed fighting in the war. His wife found out about his death while she lay in her hospital bed after giving birth to their son.

Kalsu was recognized by the Pro Football Hall of Fame in Canton, Ohio, in 1977. The plaque in his honor bears this inscription: "No one will ever know how great a football player Bob might have been, but we do know how great a man he was to give up his life for his country." His grave marker is inscribed with a quote from the Bible that reads, "There is no greater love than this; to lay down one's life for one's friends."

A forward operating base in Iraq was named after him. The University of Oklahoma "O" Club (OSU's former letterman's organization) and his teammates also celebrate his memory with a scholarship given annually to student-athletes who have completed their eligibility. The Bob Kalsu Award is given out for courageous effort.

Waddy Young

Walter "Waddy" Young was an All-America end in 1938 and played pro ball for two years before entering the air force during World War II.

He piloted a B-24 over the North Atlantic in 1943, downing two Nazi fighter planes and attacking a submarine. Young logged over 9,000 hours flying between Canada and England. He was awarded the first ever Oak Leaf Cluster for the Air Medal for distinguished service. While flying a B-29 against the Japanese, his plane, called "Waddy's Wagon," was featured in an April 1945 *National Geographic* magazine article.

On January 9, 1945, Young had completed a bombing run over Tokyo when he noticed a friend's plane from his squadron had lost an engine and was under attack by Japanese fighter planes. Young circled back to help, but both planes were lost over the Sea of Japan. Walter "Waddy" Young was only 28 years old.

OKLAHOMA RECRUITS...NOT!

The great majority of talent on the Longhorns comes from Texas itself. Not so much in Oklahoma. Because the Sooner State is so devoid of good football players, they have to cajole, lure, over-promise, and kidnap athletes to come to OU.

Of the 26 recruits in their 2012 class, 23 are from out of state. This is a far cry from the days of Coach Bud Wilkinson. During his tenure with the Sooners, Wilkinson barely recruited outside of the state of Oklahoma, preferring players from high schools around Norman.

The 2012 recruiting class even has seven Texas traitors who left the Lone Star State to play for OU.

Here's an even more telling example of the suckitude of football talent in Oklahoma. Of the 76 players on their 2011 roster, only 19 hail from in state. The others breakdown like this: six are from Kansas, four are from California, two are from New Mexico, two are from Florida, two are from Missouri, and one apiece are from Georgia and South Dakota. This leaves a whopping 39 from Texas! In other words, Texans make up 51 percent of the entire Oklahoma Sooners roster! Which explains why they win a game every now and then.

3

OKLAHOMA ODDITIES
(BESIDES THEIR OFFSPRING)

JUST WHAT THE HELL IS A SOONER?

This part of the book is for those of you from outside the state of Oklahoma—because if you don't know what a Sooner is, then you're definitely not one. (Consider yourself lucky.)

As everyone knows, only OU uses this nickname, and for good reason.

A little history is necessary here. The Land Run of 1889 occurred when the federal government—on a lark or a three-day bender or both—opened up the Oklahoma Territory for land ownership. People came from all over the world to grab a piece of turf. Remember, this was 1889—very few humans had even seen a photograph of Oklahoma, much less traveled there. This historical event actually became the focal point of the film *Far and Away* starring Nicole Kidman and Tom Cruise. If you were disappointed by that movie, just imagine how the real settlers felt back in 1889! At least you were able to leave the theater and go home to some form of civilized life. Those poor bastards were stuck in Oklahoma.

The Land Run, which opened up about two million acres, was scheduled to happen on both a specific date (April 22, 1889) and at a specific time: high noon. So over 50,000 prospective pioneers/suckers lined up in different areas of the state. In Fort Reno, they were supposed to "go" when they heard the boom of a cannon. At other starting points they were supposed to wait until a shot was heard, or a bugle, etc. The settlers who followed these rules were called *Boomers*. But some folks didn't wait for the boom, and instead left early. These individuals were called *Sooners*. It was the largest example in history of being offside, and explains why OU players are so prone to earning this penalty.

The Boomer name, however, was actually being used even before the cannon showed up. Those who wanted the territory opened up for settlers had been lobbying Congress for years. These people were called Boomers, too (as well as a few other choice words we cannot print).

Inspired by a pep club called the Sooner Rooters, the school's teams began to be called the Sooners around 1908. For about 10 years before that, the teams were known as the Rough Riders or the Boomers. The Rough Riders name came from all the Oklahoma volunteers who signed up to fight with Teddy Roosevelt's cavalry regiment in Cuba during the Spanish-American War of 1898. You see, it only took them nine years to figure out that they'd rather be shot at in Cuba than have to live in peace in Oklahoma.

THE SOONER SCHOONER MASCOT

OU can boast of having the most unique and colorful mascot in all of college football. (No one believes these boasts, or even listens to them, but they can still make them.)

The official mascot of the University of Oklahoma is the Sooner Schooner, which is a horse-drawn wagon that hurtles across the field at breakneck speed to lead the team and get the crowd revved up (when the horses aren't too drunk). This questionable vehicle is a Conestoga—a reproduction of the type of late 1800s covered wagon that many pioneers used to enter the Oklahoma Territory during the liquor-induced Land Run.

Two white ponies named Boomer and Sooner lead the wagon onto the field every time the Sooners score. It's not much to see, but it seems to get the Okies fired up. It came out so fast during one game that it actually tipped over. Thankfully, Boomer and Sooner were not hurt (their alcohol consumption had loosened them up).

The Sooner Schooner has been OU's official mascot since 1980 and has been rolling around since 1964. Before then it was used as the main transportation system in Norman.

When not thrilling the crowd at Owen Field, Boomer and Sooner relax at the Bartlett Ranch in Sapulpa with some mimosas and Bloody Mary mix. The Ruf/Neks, the school's all-male spirit squad, keep the Schooner in peak condition and drive it onto the field (when the horses are sober enough to stand).

In 2008 Fox Sports named the Sooner Schooner the third-best mascot in college football. Of course they are biased, since the Fox guys and the ponies are drinking buddies.

The Schooner got a penalty during the 1985 Orange Bowl during what is now known as the "Sooner Schooner Game." The Sooners thought they had kicked a field goal during the third quarter, but it was negated by a penalty. Sadly, nobody told those drunk horses, and so out they came, charging onto the field towing that damn wagon behind them, and ram-rodding (or should I say horse-rodding) straight through the Washington Huskies defense. So another penalty was added on, and OU had to try the field goal from 20 yards further back. It was blocked, and the Huskies went on to the upset win.

One Sooner cheerleader was hanging out of the back, waving a huge flag in the faces of the UW players. Washington's Jim Rodgers would later tell Dawgman.com, "In high school my dad had sternly warned me about throwing tantrums, that he would never let me play another down of football again if I ever lost my temper on the field. That thought raced through my head. And it was the only thing that kept me from reaching up, grabbing that damn flag, and yanking it and that little bastard right out of the wagon!"

In 2005, after a three-year study, OU introduced two other mascots, also named Boomer and Sooner. Remember, Sooners love and need repetition. But let *me* repeat something here: it took *three years* for them to study this little project. Now I know why so many OU grads go into government work.

These costumed mascots fill the need for more mobile and smaller representations of the school who can spread pride and cheer at events around the state. Or maybe school officials were just tired of Sooners fans buggering the real horses.

MEX THE DOG AND LITTLE RED

Besides horses and costumed students, can you name another legendary representation of OU school pride in animal form?

If you said Mex the Dog, you're a big enough fan to ride in the Sooner Schooner. (Just remember to bring the liquor, because ole Boomer and Sooner get a little jittery without a snort.)

Back in the early days of Oklahoma football and baseball, there weren't a lot of fences and security guards around to stop the riff raff from interfering with the games. Today these folks are just called Sooners fans, but back then they actually had a problem with stray dogs wandering into the action.

That's where Mex the Dog comes into the story. Beginning in 1915 and going all the way to 1928, Mex, a Boston terrier, patrolled the sideline in his swank red sweater with a red letter *O* on its side.

Mex got his name legitimately, since he was a Mexican *perro*. He was found in 1914 by a medic from the U.S. Army during the chaos caused by that month's Mexican Revolution. Mott Keys was the medic's name, and he found Mex in a litter of abandoned puppies just across the border from Laredo. His company adopted Mex, and he later went home to Hollis, Oklahoma, with Keys.

Since he already had experience as a mascot, and work visas were optional, Mex had no problem landing the job of team mascot for the Sooners. He resided at the Kappa Sigma frat house when not on patrol. Mex would bark for joy at every OU touchdown and home run, and soon he was the most famous canine in the state. He was more popular than the governor. Heck, he was also better-spoken than the governor.

Mex was once scheduled to travel by rail with the team to Des Moines, Iowa, for a game against Drake. But when the squad switched cars in Arkansas City, Kansas, Mex somehow managed to miss the connection. Maybe he was enjoying those famous bathtubs Arkansas City was known for in those days.

The team was disconsolate at the loss of Mex and lost the game 28–0. The *Arkansas City Traveler* printed a headline on October 28, 1924, that read "Crushing Defeat of Bennie Owen's Team is Charged to Loss of Their Mascot Here." Heads hung low on the trip back to Norman, and a 50¢ reward was posted.

Joyfully, Mex was discovered safe and sound, roaming the train platform in Arkansas City. (No word on whether or not he looked like he'd had a bath recently.) Three Oklahoma graduates traveled up to Kansas to retrieve Mex, then drove him to their next game against Oklahoma A&M in Stillwater.

Mex passed away on April 30, 1928, and the school shut down to mourn. A funeral was held on May 2. He was buried in a small casket under the stadium and remains there to this day.

Between 1953 and 1971, a student would dress up in Native American costume and attend games under the name "Little

Red." Even in Nixon-era Oklahoma, this was considered a little backward.

SONGS and CHEERS

The Boomer Sooner Fight Song has an unusual origin, with parents in both Connecticut and the Carolinas. (Unlike most Oklahomans, the fight song knows both of them.)

A student by the name of Arthur Alden wrote the lyrics in 1905. He took the tune from the song "Boola Boola," which is used at Yale. In 1906 the song was combined with North Carolina's "I'm a Tarheel Born" song. Here are the world-famous lyrics:

> *Boomer Sooner, Boomer Sooner*
> *Boomer Sooner, Boomer Sooner*
> *Boomer Sooner, Boomer Sooner*
> *Boomer Sooner, OK U!*
> *Oklahoma, Oklahoma*
> *Oklahoma, Oklahoma*
> *Oklahoma, Oklahoma*
> *Oklahoma, OK U!*
> *I'm a Sooner born and Sooner bred*
> *And when I die, I'll be Sooner dead*
> *Rah Oklahoma, Rah Oklahoma*
> *Rah Oklahoma, OK U!*

Notice all the repetition? The Okies obviously don't.

Who can help but feel their heart fill whenever the Pride of Oklahoma Marching Band forms the *OU* on the field while playing "Boomer Sooner"? Well, about 99 percent of the human race, but it's big news in Okieland.

You hear "go-go" and you know the game is about to begin. (Either that or a cop is telling you to move along.) The tradition of having a pep band perform at the football games goes all the way back to 1901, when a few people from town joined together to form the first such squad (because there was absolutely nothing else to do in Norman after the pigs were slopped).

The band is now 300 strong. And it's not just the football team that has its superstitions and traditions—the band gives them a run for their money.

While waiting in the tunnel before entering the field before home games, the trombone players scrape their horns on a concrete beam with the word *Pride* written on it. It's not very conducive to having a dent-free and shiny horn, but sacrifices have to be made for the sake of victory and a good performance. (Too bad those sacrifices so often come to naught.)

The band ends every rehearsal with "Boomer Sooner." (Once again, repetition.) On the field they break into "Oklahoma," and the songs keep coming throughout the game—"Boomer Sooner," the "OU Chant," and "OK Oklahoma," which has a unique origin itself.

"OK Oklahoma" debuted December 1, 1939, and you can hear it these days as the Sooner Schooner rolls onto the field after every extra point. The song had an unusual origin. In 1939

Fred Waring was a famous bandleader with a national radio show. (If his name sounds familiar, it might be because he's also responsible for the blender you may have sitting in your kitchen.) If a university could come up with enough signatures on a petition, Waring would arrange to have a fight song written for the school. To get the arrangement from Waring, the band promised to smoke only Chesterfield cigarettes, which was the sponsor of his radio show. (You don't want to know what they had to do for Waring to get some free chewing tobacco.)

The OU Chant came to be in 1936 when it was written by faculty member Jessie Lone Clarkson Gilkey, who was the leader of the ladies glee club. (Gilkey was also a collector of names.) If you are associated with the University of Oklahoma, you should stand and raise one finger to the sky in a vast display of unity whenever you hear this played. (You should also get over your aversion to soap.)

The Pride of Oklahoma may be the only marching band ever credited with a win on the field. During the Bedlam Series of 1983 in Stillwater, the Sooners were losing 20–3 when band director Gene Thrailkill was escorted off the field by police because he didn't have his sideline pass. The angry director instructed his band to keep playing music until OU was ahead. So play they did, regaling the fans with "Boomer Sooner" over 300 times until the Sooners took a 21–20 lead. Coach Barry Switzer gave the band credit for the come-from-behind win and even awarded them with the game ball. (Local doctors were also pleased by the upturn in business due to the hundreds of band members who needed to have their instruments surgically removed from their lips.)

The OU Yell came about at the same time football was getting its start in Norman. In 1895 it was thought that the yell that Kansas fans did was short and to the point, so OU got the same treatment:

> *Hi rickety whoop-te-do*
> *Boomer Sooner, Okla-U!*
> *Hi rickety whoop-te-do*
> *Boomer Sooner, Okla-U!*

Short. To the point. Easy to remember. And most importantly, repetitious.

COLORS AND UNIFORMS

The official colors of the Sooners are crimson and cream—which is really just a fancy way of saying red and white.

In 1895 it was decided that the school needed official colors, so university leaders turned to the faculty member with the most fashion sense, as well as the only woman on staff, Miss May Overstreet. She headed a committee that chose the colors. To her death, she denied getting the inspiration for the color scheme from a plate of raw bacon.

There have been six official helmet styles since the modern OU helmet was introduced in 1946. This may be the first example of the word *modern* being used in reference to OU.

The first one lasted for 11 very successful seasons, being used during national title runs in 1950, 1955, and 1956, as well as for 11 conference crowns. (Makes you wonder why they would change, especially considering their reliance on repetition.) It was white—sorry, cream—with a red stripe from the forehead to the nape of the neck.

The second edition of the helmet appeared in 1957, although it was basically the same save the addition of red numbers on the sides (not exactly a riot-inducing change). This version lasted for nine years and saw four conference championships, but no national ones.

Many changes were going on in the country during 1966, some rather radical, and Norman was no exception to this trend. (They even added sidewalks downtown!) A new helmet with a vastly different look also debuted that year, along with new coach Jim Mackenzie. The new helmet was mostly red, with the biggest change being the first appearance of the now-infamous interlocking *O* and *U* in round, white script. Coach Mackenzie also had small white numbers added to the back of the helmets.

This style lasted for only one season. In 1967 the OU logo changed from being round to the blockish letters that appear today. This helmet was worn for two national championships, in 1974 and 1975.

It was 1976 when the red on the helmet morphed into deep crimson—or the color of dried blood. Before that year the players were allowed to wear gray or white face masks, but in 1976 they became all white. This was the longest-lasting style, going for 24 seasons and a national championship in 1985.

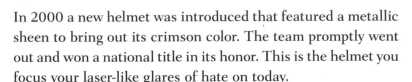
In 2000 a new helmet was introduced that featured a metallic sheen to bring out its crimson color. The team promptly went out and won a national title in its honor. This is the helmet you focus your laser-like glares of hate on today.

GAYLORD FAMILY– OKLAHOMA MEMORIAL STADIUM

The University of Texas at Austin and the University of Oklahoma both named their stadiums in honor of the brave American servicemen and women who have given their lives in war. UT later added the name of legendary football coach Darrell K. Royal to its stadium's name. The University of Oklahoma also named its stadium in honor of a special part of their history, a family named Gaylord.

So who are the Gaylords? Edward K. Gaylord and his family have given both time and money to the university. Their estimated contributions of over $50 million led to their name being added to the stadium. (There's been talk of changing the name of the state, too.)

Stroll along the east side of the Norman campus and you'll find yourself walking up to the Gaylord Family-Oklahoma Memorial Stadium (and brushing aside cobwebs). Here you'll get the feeling that you're walking into history. And you are correct, since the structure was built in 1923 and the red brick walls evoke an era of leather helmets, three yards, and a cloud of dust. (And since most Okies are still stuck in the 1930s, it still seems modern to them.)

Once you enter the largest arena in Oklahoma, you quickly see it's a little more up-to-date inside. The indoor latrines are your first clue. OU fans are so enamored with these newfangled devices that they're thinking about putting them in the state capitol, as well. And who knows, after that, maybe they'll even start to appear in some of those big fancy homes over in Oklahoma City!

The OU stadium is indeed the largest arena in the state, with more than 82,000 seats. It even holds more fans than the state prison—but just barely. An attendance record was set on November 5, 2011, when more than 85,000 fans jammed into the arena to see OU embarrass Texas Tech 41–25. (Now there was an event the folks at MENSA might overlook.) On that night, the stadium became the fourth-largest population center in the state. It was as if the entire city of Broken Arrow showed up for the game. (Which they did, and which is why every house in that town was burgled that same night.)

The Sooners are 360–79–15 in their stadium. The first game played there was on October 20, 1923, against Washington of Missouri, a 63–7 win for Oklahoma. (I guess there was no local high school available.)

While the stadium has been in the same place since Calvin Coolidge was president, the field has not. If you wanted to play in the exact spot the players played back then, you'd have to float about six feet above the ground. That's because in 1949, the playing surface was lowered six feet (the same depth you'd bury a corpse) in order to create more seating. Seems fitting, since so many OU fans' dreams die there.

PLAY LIKE A CHUMPION

Before the players run out of the locker room onto Owen Field, they pass under a sign that reads "EXIT." But right after that, they run under another sign that reads "Play Like A Champion Today." Coaches and players alike make sure to reach up and touch this totem.

No one really seems to know when this tradition began, although it was already in place during Bud Wilkinson's time as coach. The sign was originally placed 15 feet above the floor, but this caused too many players to pull their hamstrings trying to touch it, so they lowered the sign. But when too many players tripped over the sign, they moved it again, this time to its present location just above their heads.

As the players enter the field, they pass under a banner of crimson with flags on the sides representing the team's seven national titles. The fans see "Oklahoma Sooners" on their side of the banner, the players see "Play Like a Champion" on their side. Do I need to mention the repetition theme anymore? So what do the players touch when they're playing on the road? To answer this, I refer you to lyrics from The Beatles' song "With a Little Help from My Friends": "What do you see when you turn out the light? / I can't tell you, but I know it's mine."

4

WE HATE OKLAHOMA COACHES

BOB STOOPS to NEW LOWS

When Bob Stoops came to Norman in 1999, it had been four years since Oklahoma had a bowl game appearance. More than 100 wins later, the bowl games are back, even if the wins in them aren't.

OU had been known as a great rushing team for decades. In the tradition of the great Bennie Owen, Stoops showed them that the forward pass could actually be their friend, as well.

Since Stoops took over, the Sooners have set records for passing and receiving in a career, a season, and a single game. And he didn't forget the rushing legacy; they've also set a team record for rushing in a single season, with seven players having rushed for over 1,000 yards in a season. (He's done nothing to improve their collective IQ, however.)

Stoops' teams won 20 straight at one point, and none of those opponents were cream puffs—all were in Division I-A. (Sorcery is suspected.) In 2008 Stoops' 12–2 squad set a modern-day record for scoring with over 700 points. Quarterback Sam Bradford won the Heisman Trophy, following QB Jason White

Oklahoma Sooners head coach Bob Stoops has led his football teams to four national championship games since taking over the program in 1999. He's won all but the last three of them.

in 2003. Stoops also became the fastest coach to win 100 games since Teddy Roosevelt was in the White House. (To celebrate this achievement, he promptly charged up San Juan Hill.)

Stoops has led OU to four national championship games, with his 2000 team winning the national title with a 13–0 record.

He is the first coach in Sooners history to lead his first three teams to bowl games. But you may have noticed that while he's won a national title game, he's also lost three of them—his last three. (Ugly.) There was a national petition being passed around trying to ban the Sooners from ever appearing in another title game, but it was scrapped when Ohio State superseded them in national title game ineptitude.

Stoops is 139–34 for a .803 winning percentage as of January 2012. He's 8–5 against Texas, having won five in a row at one point. (Even a blind pig finds a truffle now and then. But in Oklahoma, they think they're just smelly mushrooms anyway, so they throw them away.)

BARRY SWITZER SUCKS

Many thought it might be hard to replace Chuck Fairbanks. Unfortunately for UT fans, the next man not only replaced him, but also exceeded him. Barry Switzer became the winningest coach in OU history. He was also the one who convinced Fairbanks to make the risky move to the wishbone offense in 1970.

But Switzer's tenure got off to a rocky start when the NCAA forced the team to forfeit games because of violations that occurred under Fairbanks. Switzer rebounded, however, leading the Sooners to three national titles, 12 Big 8 championships, and eight bowl victories, winning 28 straight games at one point. He also coached running back Billy Sims to the 1978 Heisman Trophy, and his teams averaged 32 points a game while holding their opponents to only 12. During one three-year period in the mid-1980s, Switzer's teams went

33–3, with all three losses coming to the Hurricanes, the only team that could beat them.

But despite this success, 1988 became a year to forget as probation once again reared its head and Switzer's chickens came home to roost. His house was even robbed by one of his own players/recidivists.

This self-proclaimed "Bootlegger's Boy" from a poor Arkansas family would go on to write a bestselling autobiography and coach the Dallas Cowboys to a Super Bowl win in 1995 over the Steelers. He is one of only two men to have coached teams to both a college national championship and a Super Bowl win. The other is his old Razorback teammate Jimmy Johnson. Talk about falling into a pile of shite and coming out smelling like a rose.

Switzer had a winning record against other legendary coaches, including Bobby Bowden, Woody Hayes, Joe Paterno, and Tom Osborne. He was 157–29–4 overall for a .837 winning percentage. He was 9–5–2 against the Longhorns, dominating Darrell Royal by some stroke of luck with three wins and one tie. He entered the College Football Hall of Fame in 2002 (but was promptly asked to leave by security).

BUD WILKINSON WHINES

Bud Wilkinson thought that players from around the Oklahoma area were all he really needed to win, and he proved that from 1947 to 1963. National titles in 1950, 1955, and 1956 were the crowning jewels of his career, which included a record 47 straight wins and a 74-game streak of conference game victories. He also coached 1952 Heisman Trophy winner Billy Vessels.

OU earned twelve consecutive conference championships under Wilkinson. When he left to run for the United States Senate, only seven other coaches at the Division One-A level had more victories. However, he was not able to win political office.

Wilkinson's 1949 team went undefeated, and spanked Louisiana State 35–0 in the Sugar Bowl despite the Tigers sending a player named "Piggy" to spy on Oklahoma. (I don't know about you, but to me, the pig is not exactly an emblem of stealth.) OU did not win the national title, however, as voters chose Notre Dame instead even though that school was too chicken to play in a bowl game.

Wilkinson's teams were so good that OU President George Cross said he "would like to build a university of which the football team would be proud." He could have run Ohio State during Jim Tressel's reign.

And Wilkinson wasn't too shabby as a player at Minnesota either. As an All-America guard, he helped his team to three straight national titles from 1934 to 1936. He was also a veteran of the navy, having served during World War II.

After a second career as a TV analyst and a stint as a member of President Richard Nixon's White House staff, Wilkinson returned to coaching in 1978 with the NFL's St. Louis Cardinals. His time there, however, was short-lived and not very successful.

Wilkinson's record at Norman was 145–29–4 for a .826 winning percentage. But he was only 9–8 against Texas despite winning six in a row against the Longhorns during the 1950s.

OTHER COACHES IN SORDID SOONERS HISTORY

The 20th century—and, more importantly, the Red River Shootout—began on an inauspicious note for Oklahoma with a 28–2 loss in Austin in 1900 under coach Fred Roberts. This was the only game all season in which OU allowed a point.

Roberts had been a star running back at Oklahoma in 1899 and took over as coach in 1901, but lasted for only one season. He left because he said he didn't agree with them playing bigger or smarter schools, but his 3–2 record might have had something to do with it, as well. Losing to UT not once but twice—in Austin to begin the season and at Norman to end it—didn't make him popular around Norman, either. Losing to Texas does not make for either a successful or long tenure at OU.

A new coach, Texas alumnus Mark McMahon, did not immediately pay dividends, as the Sooners fell to UT again to begin the 1902 season. However, that year did see the first OU game played at the Texas State Fair Grounds in Dallas—but it was not against UT. The squad lost to the Dallas Athletic Club. McMahon would pick up the pieces and lead OU to five wins and just one loss for the rest of the season.

The Sooners have five head coaches in the College Football Hall of Fame, and the first one to show up in Norman was Bennie Owen. The playing field is known as Owen Field in

honor of Benjamin G. "Bennie" Owen, who began the winning football tradition at OU. (Yup, that's right, he's the man
to blame.)

Football had been around for 10 years in Norman, but wins
over quality teams had been hard to come by before Owen
showed up in 1905. Coach Owen started off 7–2 and never
looked back, although for his first two years he returned to
Kansas during the off-season to run his restaurant. (Yes, I'll
say it: OU was cheap back then. Or maybe Owen just preferred slinging hash in Kansas to living in Norman?) Finances
were soon found to keep him around yearlong.

For the next 22 years, Owen's teams went undefeated four
times. No other man has had a longer tenure as coach of the
Sooners. (Or could stand the smell that long.) Coach Owen
would compile 122 wins with only 54 losses. That's a .677
winning percentage for you non-ciphering readers and Sooners (but I repeat myself). His teams would average almost
27 points per game while holding their opponents to only 7.
Owen's 1914 squad led the country in scoring, and the undefeated 1918 team outscored the opposition 278–7.

His squads were known for their speed and daring, often
using smaller yet quicker players to run rings around the bigger boys. (The Okies were smaller due to supplementing their
meager diet with dirt.) He especially loved the newfangled forward pass. And he made use of the "hurry-up" offense decades
before it came into vogue. When he played, he was in such
a hurry that he would start calling the next play while still
untangling from the pile after a tackle. (Don't let Drew Brees
hear about this.)

Owen was also OU's athletics director from 1907 to 1934, and led the construction of Memorial Stadium. Amazingly, he did all this with one arm tied behind his back or, more to the point, with only one arm. Owen added the responsibilities of A.D. in 1907 after losing an arm in a hunting accident that October.

Coach Owen was among the original class of inductees into the College Football Hall of Fame in 1951, along with Knute Rockne and Walter Camp. He enjoyed watching the Sooners until the age of 74. But he lived to the ripe old age of 94.

Before Bennie Owen, some rather interesting characters came to coach in Norman. Maybe the most colorful was the very first one, Jack Harts, back in 1895.

John A. "Jack" Harts not only came up with the idea of introducing football at OU, he recruited the players for the first team and, when they got injured, he was even the one to fix them up at a local barber shop on West Main Street owned by Bud Risinger. It was at this very place of business that Harts supposedly said, "Let's get up a football team." It's a scene reminiscent of a Mickey Rooney–Judy Garland, "Hey, let's put on a show" kind of movie.

When he first showed up at OU, Harts was first planning on being a student, but was also going to teach a class on elocution. (For you Sooners, that means he taught people how to speak well.) He must have used those linguistic skills to convince everyone else in the barbershop that football was a good idea. Because he could kick a ball farther than anyone on the team, and because he was such a likeable guy, Harts was chosen as the team captain and the coach.

Like many players of his day, Harts had also played at another school, Southwestern College in Kansas. But the day before the first game, he hurt his knee in practice, so he concentrated on coaching. The team was still two players short, so Harts improvised in true frontier spirit and got a horse driver and Risinger, the town barber, to suit up.

Unfortunately for them, they lost their only game—and it wasn't even a close shave. Their spirit was not rewarded on the gridiron. Not only did they not score any points, they never even achieved a first down in a loss to the Oklahoma City town team, 34–0. According to Sooners historian and OU director of sports publicity Harold Keith, "Old-timers say the only difference between this event and Custer's Massacre, which had occurred only 19 years earlier, was that in the football game there were survivors from both sides." One and done was Harts' motto for that season. Shortly after the loss, he scampered off to prospect for gold in the Yukon.

Or so it was thought. Decades later he was tracked down by Keith, who was writing a book about the early history of Oklahoma football. Keith discovered that it may not have been just gold that Hart was looking for in the frozen north. He was also searching for oil—but not the kind that comes from a gusher. Harts was looking for the oil from the head of a leviathan—he worked on a whaling ship in 1897. Indeed, his life post-Norman was anything but normal, including coal mining and politics. He survived not only a California earthquake but also dodged a tornado near Shawnee, which made much more of a fuss than the quake, according to Harts.

In his first letter back to Keith, Harts referred to himself as "the Daddy of football at the University of Oklahoma." He was extremely proud of the tradition he and his little band of pioneers had started. However, the loss of his only game at OU seemed to grow even scarier to him over the years, since he remembered the final score as being 64–0, almost twice as bad as every other record shows. But he swears it was stamped on his memory.

While living in Los Angeles in the early 1930s, Hart wrote to Keith about the local team, the Trojans, and how impressed he was with their teamwork. And once, 35 years after his playing days had ended, the old coach was sitting in the L.A. Coliseum watching USC play Notre Dame when just before a play, he heard someone near him in the stands yell out, "Let John Harts kick it!" After the shock wore off, Harts realized it was an old friend from Kansas that he hadn't seen in decades.

As for the uniforms worn back in 1895, Harts told Keith they bought 11 brown overalls, cut them off at the knees, then got a "mother, sister, or sweetheart" to pad them up front like a quilt.

OU's official website ends this legend's story with a note stating there is no Internet search or record at the university showing when Coach Harts passed away, or if he ever fulfilled his dream of returning to Norman for one more game. A search of Ancestry.com shows he probably died on August 24, 1947, but gives no word on where. As for Coach Jack Harts ever seeing another Sooners game, maybe he's watching Memorial Stadium right now. (Hopefully he's looking down, not up.)

Vernon Parrington became head coach in 1897 after trying his hand at another contact sport: politics. He ran as a populist, but wasn't popular enough to win office.

Parrington was the first fulltime head coach in Norman, but it wasn't his main calling. He's probably the only former head college football coach in America to win a Pulitzer Prize for a book on politics.

In 1897 he used his knowledge of Eastern football gained at Harvard to coach the team to a 16–0 revenge win over the Oklahoma City town team that had embarrassed them in 1895. Parrington was extremely proud of this win, as he expressed in a school magazine he published called the *Umpire*, in which he spoke of his boastful and confident opponent:

> They came from the little town up the way in special coaches, and bearing brand new canes nicely trimmed in crimson and black, and a huge banner and little "tooters" likewise trimmed in best quality all-silk ribbon. Moreover, they had several new yells they had practiced the entire 18 miles of the way and which they had learned to give, so it is reported by the trainsmen, in a very sweet ladylike and gentlemanlylike way. But alas! The horns remained untooted and the "lovely new yells" remained unyelled and the black and crimson banner drooped most dismally on its pole; the day that was so bright at three o'clock was dark and gloomy for them at four. By "them" of course is meant our friends

from Oklahoma City, who came down to see the varsity lads
taken into camp.

Parrington left coaching to teach in 1901, but stayed on as
athletics director. For the next seven years he taught lan-
guages, but politics was not through with him yet. He was
fired, along with the school president, when another political
party took over the state government, so he moved on to teach
at the University of Washington.

Parrington decided to take a trip to England in 1929, the first
vacation of his life. Perhaps he should have stayed on the job
instead—for he died suddenly in Gloucestershire.

Fred Roberts was a great halfback who was also the coach in
1901. The *Dallas Morning News* once used the word *prettiest*
to describe his play against the Longhorns. This was obviously
in the infancy of sports writing, since no sportswriter worth
his ilk would use that word to describe a football player today,
even a Sooner. Imagine if *Denver Post* columnist and ESPN
contributor Woody Paige reported that Chicago Bears and former OU defensive tackle Tommie Harris' play was the "prettiest" on the field. He'd be laughed out of the locker room. And
he'd have some explaining to do to Mr. Harris.

Roberts lasted only one year as coach because he had chores
to do on his farm. Seriously, that's why he left.

In 1902 Oklahoma needed a coach and Mark McMahon
needed a job. The former Texas player with the walrus mus-
tache also needed to pay off debts racked up during law school.
So when his current team, a railroad squad from Dallas, beat

OU during the first game they ever played at the Texas State Fair, McMahon heard about the open coaching position and applied, despite being a former Longhorn.

The powers that be in Norman decided to overlook that handicap in their eyes, and hired him on the condition that he teach them the trick play the railroad workers had used to beat them, something called the wing shift.

McMahon also played in some games, and he was needed, since at one point they played 12 games in only eight weeks. All but two of those games were played on the road. (Literally—a road.)

McMahon quickly paid off his tuition debt and left to practice law in 1903. He may be known best for bringing the first tackle dummy to the practice field in Norman, a man named Joe. He was also known for having the cojones to wear a Texas jersey in a Sooners photo.

Fred Ewing came next in 1904. But he was only a one-year stopgap, having taken a year off from medical school in Chicago to coach the team. Despite his short term, Ewing was there for several firsts. His team was the first from OU to play Oklahoma A&M, later to be called Oklahoma State. Oklahoma destroyed the boys from Stillwater 75–0. His squad was also the first to play UT at the Texas State Fair in Dallas. That didn't go so well, however, as they lost 50–10.

But the main thing Coach Ewing may be remembered for came from his medical background. He started using tape to bandage and wrap up sore or sprained ankles years before most trainers around the country made this a standard practice.

True to his word, the very day after the Thanksgiving game, Ewing headed back to Illinois to become a doctor.

Adrian Lindsey was just a .500 coach at Oklahoma from 1927 to 1931, but he is known for a few things.

Lindsey played minor league baseball before coming to Norman, and in 1931 he became the first coach to take a team from middle America all the way to Hawaii, beating the islanders 7–0. He also served in the army during World War II, retiring as a colonel in 1954.

Lewie Hardage was coach from 1932 to 1934, and is best known for his inventiveness off the field more than on it.

He devised a new uniform, half the weight of the old one, with foam rubber as the helmet, shin guards, and knee pads. While it made his team faster, it did open the players up to some ribbing from other teams because Hardage made them wear short pants that didn't even make it to the knee. The pants were as short as his tenure in Norman.

Lawrence "Biff" Jones was only at OU from 1935 to 1936, but he earned the gratitude of all future Sooners by installing needle showers and whirlpool baths. He even got a paved road built between Norman and Oklahoma City.

Jones was a lieutenant serving in France during World War I. He returned home to coach Army in 1926. He was also head coach at LSU before being fired by Louisiana's infamous governor Huey Long, who became miffed at Biff for not allowing him to give a halftime speech to the Tigers. He later went on to a successful career as head coach of Nebraska—but everyone has their faults.

Tom Stidham was a very colorful coach from 1937 to 1940. He only lost to Texas once during his four seasons. Stidham was extremely proud of his lucky gray suit, which he wore during their undefeated regular season of 1938. For 10 victories he wore the suit, bringing his team to a No. 4 ranking in the Associated Press poll and their first-ever bowl game, the Orange Bowl in Miami. But after a loss of 17–0 to Tennessee, Stidham retired to his hotel room, took off his beloved lucky gray suit, and chucked it out of his fifth-floor window. This has led to an annual tradition in South Beach every New Year's called "The Dropping of the Pants." (Actually, this tradition is gleefully followed almost every night in South Beach.)

At just 5'4" and 135 pounds, Dewey Luster may go down as the smallest head coach in Oklahoma history—but he may also have been the toughest. As a 15-year-old boy, he fought a professional boxer for 10 rounds.

Known affectionately as "Snorter" because of the piglike sounds he made while boxing, Luster won Big 6 Conference titles in 1943 and 1944 and never finished below second. He was also a four-year letterman in football with the Sooners and team captain of his undefeated senior squad.

Jim Tatum was only head coach at OU for one year, 1946, but, oh, what a year it was. Tatum had a passing relationship with NCAA rules, which led to a humongous and expensive recruiting campaign. The campaign paid off, as that class produced nine All-America players.

Tatum may actually be more famous for the men he beat out to win the job. Regents passed over both Paul "Bear" Bryant and a friend of Tatum's known as Charles "Bud" Wilkinson. At least Wilkinson stayed around as an assistant that year. Bryant went on to moderate success at some school down south.

After a win in the Gator Bowl over North Carolina State, Tatum left to coach Maryland. This led to two exhales of relief by school president Dr. George Cross. First, it allowed him to hire Bud Wilkinson; second, he was rid of a coach who took an athletics department surplus of over $125,000 and turned it into a $113,000 deficit. Tatum should have been in politics— no wonder he wound up so close to Washington, D.C.

Bud Wilkinson's replacement was a man with a long tradition of serving the Sooners. Gomer—yes, Gomer—Jones was Wilkinson's line coach for 17 seasons before taking over the reigns as head coach in 1964. (Goober was tight ends coach.) Jones spent just one year at the helm before resigning to join the marines, where he starred in his own TV sitcom. Just kidding! He actually quit coaching to concentrate on being athletics director.

Eighteen players became All-Americans under Jones' tutelage. Before coaching, he played for the NFL's Cleveland Rams. Tragically, while traveling with the Oklahoma basketball team to the NIT in 1971, he collapsed and died in a New York City subway station.

Tragedy also followed Jones' replacement as head coach. After just one season in 1966, Jim Mackenzie died of a heart attack. He had come over from Arkansas, where he had devised the great Razorback defenses. Ironically, Mackenzie had been an All-SEC tackle on Bear Bryant's 1950 Kentucky team, which upset the Sooners' national title team 13–7 in the Sugar Bowl of 1951. In those days, the national champion was named before the bowl games were played.

Chuck Fairbanks entered as head coach in 1967 already a winner. He was a player on Michigan State's 1952 national title team and almost became the head coach at Tennessee. Fairbanks is best known for copycatting Texas and bringing the wishbone offense to Oklahoma. He won three Big 8 championships and coached nine All-Americans, including the 1969 Heisman Trophy winner, running back Steve Owens. He left in 1973 to coach the New England Patriots, later returning to the college ranks at Colorado.

5

WE HATE THE TITLES THE SOONERS HAVE WON (BUT LOVE THE ONES THEY'VE BLOWN)

A SHORT HISTORY OF TITLES WON

Seven national championships—just the sound of it makes you grit your teeth.

1950

The very first one was in 1950 under Bud Wilkinson in what was believed at first to be just a rebuilding year (and that was just the campus outhouse). But by the time the season ended, there were four All-Americans on this team: Jim Weatherall, Buddy Jones, Leon Heath, and Frankie Anderson all made the list. Billy Vessels was still two seasons away from his Heisman Trophy, but he did score 15 touchdowns in 1950.

The season opened with a shutout of Boston College (playing the Kennedy family in a pickup game would have been tougher at the time). Going back to the 1949 season, it was the third straight blanking of a team by the Oklahoma defense. Mule

Train Heath scored the winning touchdown at home with just 37 seconds left to beat Texas A&M in game two. Once again, however, the opponent was not exactly prime competition.

The next week the Sooners were losing by six with just four minutes left before recovering a fumble and beating Texas, 14–13. Finally, a win over a stellar opponent.

The next three games were easier as the Sooners defeated Kansas State, Iowa State, and Colorado. The K-State win was another shutout. One wonders why they didn't just schedule Vassar, as well.

But something happened against Kansas that had never before occurred with Wilkinson as head coach—the Sooners were shut out in the first half. (Must have been the collective hangover.) They found their offense in the second half and won easily.

After whipping Missouri, something else happened for the first time: Oklahoma was ranked No. 1 for the first time ever in something other than soil erosion.

A strong Nebraska team was next, and OU found itself down in the third quarter before rallying for 21 points behind the amazing feet and feats of Vessels, who ran for three touchdowns and 208 yards while also throwing a touchdown pass. (He learned to multitask from his father, who was also his uncle and his grandpappy.)

Claude Arnold threw four touchdowns the next week in a pounding of Oklahoma State, and just like that, the first national title was coming to Norman. (It cried all the way there.) In those days the title was handed out before the bowl games, which was a good thing for OU since they lost to Bear Bryant's Kentucky team 13–7 in the Sugar Bowl on New Year's Day 1951 to finish 10–1. Army came in second that year, with UT at No. 3.

1955

The second national championship came five years later in 1955. Once again the role of underdog worked in Oklahoma's favor, as they made their way up the Associated Press poll until finally reaching No. 1 during week eight. (Bribery was suspected.) That was about halfway through their record 47-game winning streak. Two All-Americans were on this squad: guard Bo Bolinger and a newcomer at halfback named Tommy McDonald. They proceeded to lead the country in scoring offense, rushing offense, and total offense. (In fact, they were very offensive to most people.)

The defense shut out five of the 10 teams they faced in the regular season. Only two opponents scored more than seven points. Look up the word *domination* in the dictionary and you will find a photo of the 1955 OU defense. (Just make sure you wash out your eyes immediately afterward.) They opened with a win over the Tar Heels. Pittsburgh was the next victim at Owen Field.

Oklahoma celebrated the 50th occurrence of the Red River Shootout with a 20–0 victory over the Longhorns. They intercepted the Horns five times, with linebacker Jerry Tubbs, who also played center, making three of the picks. It was the first

Oklahoma coach Bud Wilkinson is lifted up by his quarterback Rodger Taylor (38) and fullback Bill Brown (45) after beating Maryland 20–6 in the Orange Bowl to win the coach's second of three national championships.

time they'd shut out Texas in 17 years. (Keep moving Johnny, nothing to see here.)

OU spotted the Jayhawks six points on their opening drive the next week, then crushed them 44–6. The Kansas offense spent the rest of the game playing on their side of the field. (And on their asses.) The Buffaloes were next, and they thought they had a pretty good defense. (They also thought chocolate milk came from cows that stood in the shade.) Coach Wilkinson deployed what he called the "no recovery" offense—nowadays we call it the "no huddle." Oklahoma scored eight touchdowns that day against a Colorado team ranked 14th in the nation. The Wildcats of Kansas State would be the last team to score against OU during the regular season, but their seven measly points did not compare favorably to the Sooners' 40.

Four consecutive shutouts—over the Tigers of Missouri, the Cyclones, the Cornhuskers, and Oklahoma State—followed. Oklahoma outscored those four teams 166–0. The game against Nebraska was for the conference title, as it was done at that time. The day before the game in Lincoln, Huskers coach Bill Grassford resigned. This was like Custer resigning before Little Big Horn. If he thought this might inspire his troops, he was sadly mistaken, as they fell 41–0. It was the 10th time in a row that the Sooners had won their conference. (Remember, Texas was not part of that conference.)

This set up a New Year's Day masterpiece against Maryland, a battle of two unbeaten teams in the Orange Bowl. Oklahoma had shattered the Terrapins' hopes of a perfect season just two years before, so revenge was on the turtles' minds going into Miami. And that's where it stayed—because no revenge happened on the field of play. OU won the day 20–6. Michigan State came in second that season, and the Terps ended up third.

1956

OU didn't have to wait long for the next national championship—only one season. The 1956 Oklahoma team is considered by many to be the finest one Bud Wilkinson ever coached, if not the best in OU history. (Which would make it about equal with the 15th-best Longhorns team.)

If you think the NCAA has some stupid rules, get a load of this one: in 1956 the conference forbade a team from going to a bowl game two years in a row! Talk about Grinches.

The Sooners led the entire nation in offense for the second straight year with almost 47 points per game. The defense was none too shabby either, with six shutouts, including the first three opponents of the season. The year started with a blowout home win over UNC—literally, it was a very blustery day. The next week they set the school mark with their 32nd straight victory, a 66–0 no-doubter against K-State. UT was the last in the triumvirate of shutouts as Oklahoma embarrassed them 45–0. Clendon Thomas and Tommy McDonald each had three touchdowns.

The Jayhawks managed to score, but not near enough to upset OU. A bizarre thing happened, however; Michigan State was ranked No. 1 that week, instead of a team that had now won 34 in a row. OU is the Rodney Dangerfield of football. So they were a little miffed when they journeyed up to South Bend,

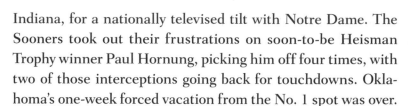

Indiana, for a nationally televised tilt with Notre Dame. The Sooners took out their frustrations on soon-to-be Heisman Trophy winner Paul Hornung, picking him off four times, with two of those interceptions going back for touchdowns. Oklahoma's one-week forced vacation from the No. 1 spot was over.

Maybe they were a little too confident going into their next game against the Buffaloes, or maybe it was another hangover, because they quickly fell behind and were down 19–6 at the half. But they kept Colorado off the scoreboard in the second half and won 27–19. No other team came as close that season (mainly due to body odor).

Iowa State was held to just 35 yards as OU wrapped up another Big 7 Conference championship. But once again the AP voters dissed Oklahoma, placing Tennessee at No. 1. And history repeated itself as the Sooners regained the top spot in just one week with a 67–14 demolishing of Missouri. It was also a special win for Coach Wilkinson. His mentor, Tigers coach Don Faurot, had announced his retirement at the end of the season—and the victory meant Wilkinson never lost to him. (He could have at least given the old man one going away present!)

A spanking of Nebraska gave OU a tie for the college record for 39 straight wins, a mark set by the Washington Huskies way back in 1914. The next week the record became Oklahoma's with a huge shutout win over Oklahoma State, 53–0. Coach Wilkinson put all his seniors in for the final drive, which came down to the 2-yard line. Guard Ed Gray looked at quarterback Jimmy Harris and told him he wanted to score a touchdown. So Gray changed places with Tommy McDonald and promptly bulled his way into the end zone for the only score of his career. Earlier in the game, Clendon Thomas scored twice to lead the country in scoring with 108 points.

Oklahoma was just the fourth team to win national titles two years in a row. Tennessee came in second that season.

There were four All-Americans on this team: guards Ed Gray and Bill Krisher, center Jerry Tubbs, and halfback Tommy McDonald. And Wilkinson had entered a plateau that has yet to be equaled in college football. He's also the only man to win three national titles as both a coach and a player. As a coach he won in 1950, 1955, and 1956. As a player with the Golden Gophers he won it in 1934, 1935, and 1936. Don Faurot had created a monster.

1974

Thankfully, almost 20 years would elapse before the next national championship, in 1974. It was a dominating defensive team that posted three shutouts that season. Four teams couldn't even find the end zone. But the offense didn't take a backseat to the defense—or anyone else, for that matter— leading the country in scoring with 43 points a game. They set an NCAA record that still stands today—almost 74 rushing attempts per game. (They learned their technique while running from campus police.)

It was the beginning of three national titles for head coach Barry Switzer, as his Sooners became the only undefeated team that season at 11–0. For the first time in 17 years, Oklahoma was ranked No. 1 to begin the season.

Baylor put up a tough fight in the opener, and a 28–11 victory was not enough to keep OU on top of the AP poll. They rebounded, however, to score 72 on Utah State. Wake Forest was the next victim, going down 63–0 with nine different Sooners scoring a touchdown. (The water boy even scored.)

Texas showed up for the big game in Dallas and actually led 13–7 in the fourth quarter. But split end Billy Brooks raced a reverse 40 yards for the game-tying score, and that's where it stood until linebacker Rod Shoate recovered a fumble at midfield. Tony DiRienzo hit a 37-yard field goal for the 16–13 win. Shoate also had 21 tackles and a forced fumble in the game, which we will not dwell upon any further.

Colorado was no problem as running back Joe Washington scampered for four touchdowns and 200 yards. Kansas State also got the Demon Deacon treatment, another 63–0 pounding. Iowa State fell next, and then the Sooners shut out a fine Missouri offense. Oklahoma was back at No. 1 to stay.

They cruised over Kansas, which set up the Nebraska game for the Big 8 championship. In the big game the offense racked up 482 yards rushing and didn't even have to complete a pass in a 28–14 victory. Defensive back Randy Hughes picked off three passes. It was their second straight Big 8 title.

Oklahoma State put up a fight in the final regular season game and had the lead late, but a five-touchdown blitz gave the Sooners a 44–13 win over the Cowboys.

Eight All-Americans led this team: linebacker Rod Shoate, halfback Joe Washington, defensive linemen and brothers

Lee Roy and Dewey Selmon, split end Tinker Owens, center Kyle Davis, guard John Roush, and defensive back Randy Hughes. Southern Cal came in second that season, and the Cornhuskers ninth.

1975

It was another short wait until the next championship, as 1975 was pretty much a repeat of 1974. Quarterback Steve Davis was the leader as a senior. He only lost one game as a Sooners starter; he may have had some heavenly help, since he was also a preacher. The defense had its share of leaders, as well, especially defensive tackle Lee Roy Selmon, who would take home both the Lombardi Award and the Outland Trophy for that season.

Oklahoma plucked the Ducks 62–7 in the opener. Oregon gave up the ball 10 times on turnovers forced by the defense. The next week they faced No. 15 Pitt with their star running back Tony Dorsett, who would win the Heisman Trophy a year later. OU handed Dorsett the worst game of his college career, with only 17 yards on 12 carries. It was Joe Washington who owned the stage that day, rushing for 166 yards and three touchdowns in a 46–10 victory.

A Friday night game in Miami proved a tough contest, but Oklahoma prevailed 20–17. An extremely tough game followed against the Buffaloes, who were undefeated and had the best offense in the college ranks. Colorado overcame a two-touchdown deficit to pull within one with a little over a minute left. Coach Bill Mallory had faith in his kicker, Tom Mackenzie—even though he had missed two field goals in the game already—and Mallory decided against going for the win with a two-point conversion. His faith was misplaced. Mackenzie missed the chip shot extra point, and Oklahoma had a 21–20 win. This was too close to impress the voters, who demoted OU to No. 2.

The Red River Rivalry featured the fleet-of-foot Washington against the pounding running style of fifth-ranked UT's Earl Campbell. Yet it was Horace Ivory who stole the spotlight with his 33-yard run for the winning touchdown in a 24–17 victory. We'll speak no further on this matter.

The next three games were cakewalks over the State teams from Kansas, Iowa, and Oklahoma, in order. The Wildcats, Cyclones, and Cowboys could only muster 17 points put together.

But then disaster struck. Hee hee! The unranked Jayhawks did a rare thing indeed: they manned up and upset OU 23–3, plummeting the Sooners to No. 6 and snapping a 28-game winning streak. It had been 37 games since Oklahoma had tasted defeat.

Things looked bleak again the next week against Mizzou, with the Tigers ranked 18th. Joe Washington once again rushed to the rescue. He scored a 71-yard touchdown run on a fourth-down play to pull the team to within a point. He then took the ball for the two-point conversion to give Oklahoma a 28–27 lead. But OU had to buckle down some more and watch Missouri miss not one, but two field-goal attempts before the victory was assured. The narrow win dropped them to No. 7 in the AP poll, and prospects for a repeat title seemed distant.

The Big 8 championship, however, was still there for the grasping against the Huskers, who came in ranked second in the nation. Nebraska showed up for the kickoff, but then left the game mentally and physically. The Sooners defense forced six turnovers for an easy 35–10 upset and another conference title, and OU moved up in the polls.

Oklahoma found itself in the Orange Bowl against the No. 5 Wolverines. Earlier that day, they had seen UCLA upset No. 1 Ohio State in the Rose Bowl in a rematch of a game in October that the Buckeyes had won handily. Barry Switzer then went out and won his first bowl game as head coach, 14–6 over Michigan. The final AP poll placed OU No. 1, making them only the fifth team to win two straight national championships, and the first to do so since the 1955–1956 Sooners. Arizona State finished second, the Longhorns sixth, and the Cornhuskers ninth.

Once again, eight Oklahoma players were All-Americans: brothers and linemen Lee Roy and Dewey Selmon, tackle Mike Vaughan, guard Terry Webb, split ends Billy Brooks and Tinker Owens, defensive end Jimbo Elrod, and halfback Joe Washington.

1985

Ten years would pass before the next national championship in 1985. The Sooners opened the season in Minneapolis against Minnesota, and the game was closer than it should have been, with Oklahoma pulling out a 13–7 win behind quarterback Troy Aikman. Their next match—another away game, this time against Kansas State—turned out to be an easy whipping.

The high-powered offense could only score 14 points against Texas, but it was enough, as the defense put together one of their greatest games ever, holding UT to negative yardage in the second half for a 14–7 win. They did it without nose guard Tony Casillas, who left the game early with a knee injury. Linebacker Brian Bosworth came up big with an interception. This is just too much to take, so we'll move on with our story.

The Sooners' first home game of the season turned out to be not so nice, as the Hurricanes upset the third-ranked Sooners 27–14 behind the strong throwing arm of Vinny Testaverde. Troy Aikman was injured in the first half and replaced by freshman quarterback Jamelle Holieway. The loss placed OU at No. 10. Two easy wins against Iowa State and Kansas followed. Holieway became a star against Missouri with 156 yards rushing and 168 passing, surpassing Sooners quarterback Jack Mildren for total offense in one game.

No. 7 Oklahoma blanked Colorado to go into the game in Norman against Nebraska ranked fifth. A 27–7 pounding of the Cornhuskers then propelled them to No. 3. The Huskers didn't even score until the last minute of the game, and only then because they picked up a fumble by the Sooners and ran it back.

The Ice Bowl was next, a frozen game in Stillwater. The schedulers picked a bad time for the first night game ever in the series, as the wind chill was around 0°F, with sleet blowing around the stadium. No. 17 Oklahoma State came about as close to scoring as a Sooner on a Saturday night, as OU won 13–0.

After a 35–13 win against SMU, the Sooners were Big 8 champions and headed to another Orange Bowl. They were ranked No. 3 in the nation but were underdogs heading into Miami to play top-ranked Penn State. This 25–10 victory was a feast for the offense, as Tim Lashar hit four field goals, Lydell Carr led with 148 yards rushing (with 61 coming on one scoring play), tight end Keith Jackson had a 71-yard touchdown catch, and Jamelle Holieway won his eighth-straight game since taking over as the signal-caller.

Meanwhile, the Canes were losing in the Sugar Bowl, which meant national championship No. 6 for the Sooners. Michigan finished second. The Nittany Lions fell to third. Three All-Americans, all on defense, led this team: linebacker Brian Bosworth, defensive end Kevin Murphy, and nose guard Tony Casillas.

2000

This brings us to the seventh—and hopefully last—national championship for Oklahoma. A new millennium of Sooners football began with a blast in 2000. The season began with an uphill climb, as OU was barely in the top 20 at No. 19 when they took the field against Texas–El Paso. A 55–14 pounding set the stage for what was to come. But despite that big win, the Sooners fell to 20th going into a 45–7 spanking of Arkansas State. That victory propelled them up three spots to 17th. Rice was devoured 42–14, and then a 14th-ranked Oklahoma took care of Kansas 34–16.

All these were warm-ups for what came next, when OU would face three top 10 teams over a three week period. Fans now call that series of games "Red October." No. 10 Texas fell first in a 63–14 upset to an 11th-ranked Sooners team. (It's too painful to even discuss at length.) The next week, a No. 8 Oklahoma upended another higher-ranked squad in second-ranked Kansas State, 41–31. The month ended with a showdown between No. 3 OU and top-ranked Nebraska. The Sooners prevailed 31–14 to become the first team in NCAA history to beat the No. 2 and No. 1 teams back-to-back. OU found themselves at No. 1 for the first time in 15 seasons.

The view from this height suited them: the crimson and cream avalanche had begun and would not be stopped. Oklahoma steamrolled Baylor 56–7, then got past 23rd-ranked Texas A&M 35–31 in front of a tough crowd in College Station, overcoming an 11-point deficit in the final quarter. It was the defense that came to the rescue: linebacker Torrance Marshall returned an interception 41 yards for the go-ahead touchdown as the defense held off a fierce Aggies offense.

Texas Tech was the next victim, falling 27–13. Oklahoma State put up a fight but still fell 12–7. This set up a rematch in the Big 12 title game against the Wildcats, now ranked eighth. Josh Heupel threw two touchdown passes and ran for another score, and Tim Duncan picked a fine time to kick his career-longest field goal with just 1:25 remaining for a thrilling 27–24 victory and the conference championship. Duncan would go on to a Hall of Fame career in the NBA. (Not really—different Timmy.)

It was on to the BCS National Championship game against a mighty Florida State Seminoles team at the Orange Bowl in Miami. Legendary coach Bobby Bowden's third-ranked team could muster no offense against the Sooners defense, and Oklahoma had national title number seven with a 13–2 win. Quentin Griffin scored the only touchdown of the game in the fourth quarter, and Tim Duncan booted two field goals. FSU was on the verge of suffering their first shutout in 12 seasons before they tackled punter Jeff Ferguson in the end zone with under a minute to play for a safety.

Heupel may have finished second to Chris Weinke for the Heisman Trophy, but the lefty made sure he wouldn't finish second that night. And just as in the pivotal game against Texas A&M, Torrance Marshall stepped up to earn Most Valuable Player honors. Three OU players made All-America: quarterback Josh Heupel, linebacker Rocky Calmus, and free safety J.T. Thatcher, a hometown kid from Norman who overcame that handicap to achieve mediocrity. The Hurricanes came in second that season, the 'Noles fifth, the Cornhuskers eighth, and Kansas State ninth. Thus ends the tale of the seven national championships of the Oklahoma Sooners—a tale of woe and money.

A MUCH MORE ENJOYABLE HISTORY OF TITLES BLOWN

Since winning the national title for the 2000 season, OU has been in three national championship bowl games—and lost all three. Let's gleefully recount each blown opportunity in grand detail. Sit back, pop open a cold one, and enjoy.

January 4, 2004, the Sugar Bowl, New Orleans

The Sooners' first chance to regain the trophy was against Louisiana State University in what was basically a home game for LSU. OU didn't come into the game without their own weapons—they had the No. 1–ranked offense in the nation, averaging 45 points per game. But Heisman Trophy winning quarterback Jason White was blitzed into oblivion by the Tigers defense, who bragged that they played real football in the SEC. The final score was 21–14 LSU, but it wasn't even that close, as the Sooners had to rely on a blocked punt by Brandon Shelby and an interception by Brodney Pool to score their only two touchdowns.

White completed 13 of 37 passes for a measly 102 yards—not exactly Heisman-worthy numbers. Oh yeah, he also tossed two picks, with one of them being run back for a score. LSU defensive end Marquise Hill derisively referred to White as "Mr. Heisman" throughout the game. Up until this game, the Sooners had averaged over 461 yards a game on offense. They managed only a pitiful 154 yards in this one. The Associated Press voted Southern Cal No. 1.

January 4, 2005, the Orange Bowl, Miami

OU only had to wait one year for the chance to efface their embarrassing loss in the national title game the previous year. They should have kept waiting.

This was supposed to be a Clash of the Titans. Southern Cal had been ranked No. 1 all season, and Oklahoma No. 2. But it was over before halftime. USC scored 14 points during the first quarter, then added 24 more in the second, and went on to destroy the Sooners 55–19 in front of a national television audience. Popeye never even beat Bluto up that badly. OU didn't help themselves, as the Trojans scored 31 points off five Oklahoma turnovers.

Unlike Jason White the year before, Matt Leinart showed what a true Heisman Trophy–winning quarterback looks like in a championship game. The lefty threw for an Orange Bowl–record five touchdowns and 332 yards with no interceptions. Three of those touchdowns went to receiver Steve Smith.

Just like the year before, White threw two picks. But he wasn't the only dipstick on the field that night for the Sooners. Early in the game, the Men from Troy punted the football down to the OU goal line. It was about to roll dead when unbelievably, Mark Bradley scooped up the ball and tried to run with it. He obviously didn't see all the Trojans waiting there to tackle him. Bradley immediately fumbled, USC recovered, scored on the next play, and never looked back.

OU running back Adrian Peterson was held to just 82 yards rushing. LenDale White ran for two touchdowns and 118 yards for the Trojans as they amassed 525 total yards against a no-show Oklahoma defense. Amazingly, both teams had the same number of first downs, while Southern Cal had three times as many penalties as OU.

Southern Cal running back Reggie Bush later said he felt sorry for the fans, saying they had paid all that money and didn't even get a chance to watch much of a game. It was the worst beating an Oklahoma team has ever taken in a bowl game. OU defensive end Larry Birdine had a heaping portion of crow to eat afterward, since he had called Leinart an over-rated quarterback on an average offense before the game.

Leinart enjoyed the experience so much that he would later choose to return for his senior season, which in retrospect may not have been the best decision. After a loss to Texas in the Rose Bowl to give the Longhorns the national championship the following year, Leinart's draft stock dropped and his NFL career has since been a major disappointment. But he was on top of the world against the Sooners that night.

Oklahoma head coach Bob Stoops summed up the debacle by saying, "We just got whipped." Yep, that about covers it.

January 8, 2009, the BCS Championship, Miami

It would be four years before OU would play in another national title game. Once again, they should have passed on the opportunity. Florida followed the Tim Tebow wave to a 24–14 win over second-ranked Oklahoma, winning their second national championship in three seasons.

Earlier in the season, a teary-eyed Tebow had shaken off an upset home loss to Ole Miss by promising his team they would not lose again that season. He then shook off a career-high two interceptions against the Sooners for the win. His final touchdown was a four-yard jump pass to David Nelson for the last score of the game.

It was a rather evenly matched game between the signal-callers. Tebow had won the Heisman Trophy the year before, and he faced the current Heisman winner, Sam Bradford. Tebow was

18-of-30 for two touchdowns and 231 yards. Bradford went 26-of-41 with two scores, 256 yards, and two picks. But Tebow ran for 109 yards, making him the player of the game. Percy Harvin rushed for a touchdown and 122 yards for the victorious Gators.

The loss was the fifth in a row in a Bowl Championship Series bowl game for Oklahoma. Despite setting a modern-day record of 702 points scored during the season, once again the offense stayed home in Norman.

Other Bowl Game Losses

Of course, those last three examples weren't the only times an OU team blew a national title game. Oklahoma came into the 1988 Orange Bowl on New Year's Day ranked No. 1 in the country. They left as losers after falling to No. 2 Miami 20–14. It was a glorified home game for the Hurricanes. The only highlight for the Sooners was a fumblerooski that went for a 29-yard touchdown.

The 1985 Orange Bowl was also not a pleasant experience for OU. They came into the game against fourth-ranked Washington as the No. 2 team in the country. Head Coach Barry Switzer was arguing in the media that the Sooners should have been No. 1 instead of Brigham Young University because Oklahoma had played a tougher schedule. His argument became moot when his team laid an egg, with the Huskies overcoming a fourth-quarter deficit to beat OU 28–17. BYU would go on to win the national championship.

The 1978 Orange Bowl was another dud for Oklahoma. Going into the game ranked No. 2 and in competition for the national title, OU was schooled by sixth-ranked Arkansas, 31–6. Head Coach Barry Switzer called it the most disappointing loss of his career. (That's saying something, since this was a man who had previously lost all integrity.)

Oklahoma doesn't just blow national title games, of course; they suck at regular bowl games, too. Take the 2008 Fiesta Bowl. (Please.) It was a BCS bowl game held in Glendale, Arizona, on January 2 against West Virginia. The Mountaineers spanked OU 48–28 before an appreciative nation. The Sooners had entered the game ranked third in the country, and WVU wasn't even in the top 10.

West Virginia quarterback Pat White made Oklahoma's defense look like they were playing flag football. White passed for two scores and 176 yards. He also scampered for 150 yards on the ground. The OU defense allowed a team-record 349 yards rushing against them in a bowl game. White also set a WVU record in a bowl game by tossing a 79-yard scoring pass to Tito Gonzales. They had 525 yards of offense against the Girl Scout troop masquerading as Oklahoma defenders. Quarterback Sam Bradford threw two touchdowns, but also gave up an interception in the end zone.

To add insult to injury, Bob Stoops was out-maneuvered by an interim coach, Bill Stewart. Stewart had stepped in for Rich Rodriguez, who had jilted his alma mater and taken a sack with a big $ sign on the side of it and ran off to Michigan. Stoops made two decisions that backfired: going for two points and an onside kick. Neither worked.

The Mountaineers did all this without the services of their best running back, as Steve Slaton was injured early in the game. But Noel Devine stepped right in, scoring two touchdowns and running for 108 yards. To make a very dated reference, Noel Coward could have rushed for 100 yards against the Sooners that night. It was their fourth loss in five bowl games, and to make matters worse (or better, if you're a Texas fan), it came on the same exact field that had seen one of their most embarrassing defeats ever a year earlier.

The 2007 Fiesta Bowl was best exemplified in this joke: Will the den mother of the Boise Cub Scout Troop please come pick up her boys? They're beating the snot out of the Oklahoma Sooners. Boise State was trying to show the nation they truly belonged in a big bowl against the big boys—well, at least against OU. BSU held Adrian Peterson to just 77 yards rushing, although he did score two touchdowns.

The Broncos jumped out to an 18-point lead before the Big 12 champions were able to rally and make it a game. In fact, the Sooners had a 35–28 lead late in the game when the Broncos pulled out some trick plays. Coach Chris Peterson rolled the dice on fourth-and-18. BSU quarterback Jared Zabransky threw a pass to Drisan James, who then turned and pitched the football to Jerard Rabb—the ole "Hook and Ladder" play. Rabb sprinted the remaining 35 yards for the touchdown. The extra point sent the game into overtime.

The Broncos found themselves losing 42–35 and down to another fourth down in overtime. This time Coach Peterson called a halfback option pass that worked for a touchdown.

But instead of just tying the game with the extra point, Peterson went for the two-point conversion with the ole "Statue of Liberty" play, in which the quarterback fades back, holds the ball up like he's going to throw it, then sneakily hands it off behind his back to a running back, in this case Ian Johnson. Johnson waltzed into the end zone for the two points and a 43–42 victory. It was one of the most thrilling upsets in bowl history and proved that Boise State could play with the big boys. (Or at least Oklahoma.)

The 1968 Bluebonnet Bowl in Houston saw the Sooners blow a 20–6 lead in the fourth quarter and fall to Southern Methodist University 28–27. Oklahoma blew an easy field goal at the end of the game that would have won it.

The 1965 Gator Bowl in Jacksonville was the ugly scene of a Florida State rout of OU, 36–19. Seminoles receiver Fred Biletnikoff had four touchdown receptions. Four of Florida State's touchdown passes came on fourth downs.

The 1963 Orange Bowl in Miami saw future NFL stars Joe Namath and Lee Roy Jordan lead Alabama to a 17–0 shutout win over the Sooners. Bear Bryant got the best of Bud Wilkinson as Oklahoma fumbled twice on first-and-goals.

The 1951 Sugar Bowl in Tulane Stadium in New Orleans was the first time The Bear and Bud hooked up against each other in a bowl game, and this 13–7 victory for Bryant was no different than the '63 Orange Bowl—except this time the Bear's team was Kentucky, making the loss even more embarrassing. And to make matters even worse for OU, they had just been awarded the national title before the embarrassing loss (back then the title was decided before the bowl games)—so No. 1 lost to No. 7.

The 1939 Orange Bowl began the seemingly annual tradition of Oklahoma being beaten in Miami. No. 4 OU and second-ranked Tennessee were both unbeaten and untied. Legendary head coach Robert Neyland's Volunteers came out 17–0 victors.

Want more? The 31–6 loss at the 1994 Copper Bowl in Tucson put an exclamation point on the worst regular season in three decades in Norman. The Clemson Tigers were 0–15 against Oklahoma before their 13–6 victory over the Sooners in the 1989 Citrus Bowl in Orlando. And the Sooners squandered Marcus Dupree's 239 yards rushing against Arizona State in the 1983 Fiesta Bowl in Tempe, losing 32–21.

THAT STUPID STREAK

Forty-seven consecutive wins. When you see it on paper, it actually doesn't seem like all that much. Does it? Yet this record, which was set between 1953 and 1957, still stands today. In major college football there have been only four streaks of 30 wins or more since 1918, and OU has two of those four (bought and paid for).

Ironically, this streak was book-ended by games with the Fighting Irish. In 1953 OU lost their season opener to Notre Dame, 28–21. Oklahoma wouldn't lose again for four years. A 7–7 tie with Pittsburgh followed that loss, and then 47 victories followed. The streak wouldn't end until the Irish beat them again, 7–0, on November 16, 1957, in Norman. OU would go

OKLAHOMA

OTHER THINGS THAT SOONERS HAVE DONE 47 TIMES IN A ROW

* ★ Failed their SAT tests
* ★ Not bathed
* ★ Not even touched water
* ★ Remained drunk
* ★ Been incarcerated on a Saturday night

on to win the rest of their games in 1957 and finish 10–1 with a win over Duke in the Orange Bowl.

The streak began with a 19–14 win over the Longhorns on October 10, 1953. Argh. That was the closest anyone came to beating Oklahoma that season. The rest of that season was a chain of uninterrupted victories, culminating in a 7–0 Orange Bowl win over the Terrapins.

Oklahoma went 10–0 in 1954, then bettered that with an 11–0 record in 1955. The closest anyone came to upsetting them in 1954 was in game two of the season, when the Horned Frogs came within five points. The 1955 season opener, a 13–6 win over the Tar Heels, was the closest anyone came to upending them that season. The January 1956 Orange Bowl win, once again over the Terps, gave the Sooners their second national title and their 30th straight victory.

A 10–0 season followed in 1956 along with a repeat national championship, putting OU's winning streak at 40 games.

Colorado came closest to ending it, but fell 27– 19. OU's 47th win, the last in the streak, came against Missouri in Columbia on November 9, 1957, a 39–14 victory.

During this amazing streak, OU scored 1,620 points while holding their opponents to just 269. They scored 86 percent of all the points scored by both teams in those contests. And the Sooners actually became more dominant as the streak continued. In 1954 they scored 304 points to just 62 for their adversaries. In 1955 that differential increased to 385 versus 60. This scoring differential came to a dramatic pinnacle in 1956, when OU scored 466 points while holding their opponents to only 51. Godzilla didn't stomp Tokyo nearly as badly!

Songwriter Ray Stevens was so impressed that he wrote a hit song called "The Streak" during the 1970s. (Actually, Stevens wrote the song about the craze for running butt naked in public, but it makes for good copy.)

A FINE HISTORY...OF CHEATING

The Oklahoma Sooners cheat. They can't help it—it's in their nature. Heck, it's even in their very name! The name Sooners refers to settlers who cheated by leaving sooner than was allowed while claiming land in the state. (But they got their just desserts when they finally saw the land they had cheated to get.)

The OU football team has been caught more times than the Hamburglar. The first official reprimand from the NCAA came all the way back in 1955. Seems some players were getting their bills paid by the school—bills such as tuition. It didn't stop at the players, either. Their families were getting money, too. (Probably to pay for cosmetic surgery.) Oklahoma received probation for the infractions.

The NCAA came visiting again in 1960, this time investigating a slush fund for players. An athletics department official tried to slow down the probe, but the NCAA still discovered that OU staffers were running the fund. (They like to keep things in-house in Norman—no outsourcing there.) The team was placed on "indefinite suspension" until they could prove the fund no longer existed. (This smacks of "double secret probation," for all the good it did.)

In 1973 an Oklahoma assistant played fast and loose with the facts on a player's transcript to make sure that he'd be eligible to play. Boosters were also caught giving cars to recruits at that time. The NCAA tends to frown on this, so they banned the Sooners from playing in a bowl game, or even on TV. (This was not such a hardship, since most Okies had yet to even hear of radio, much less own a television.)

Throughout the 1980s and Coach Barry Switzer's regime, OU players openly flaunted their expensive cars and clothes. Some even wrote about it in their autobiographies. But in 1988 the chicken came home to roost—and to talk to the NCAA. So the school administration set up their own investigation and—shockingly—found nothing amiss. The NCAA's investigation, however, revealed that assistant coaches had paid bills, provided rides, and stuffed envelopes with cash for recruits. Players had also been selling their game tickets. What was worse for OU, the players were talking. So the college investigated a second time. Surprise, surprise, as Gomer Pyle would say, once again they found no wrongdoing! If OU officials had

THINGS *A SOONER HAS* NEVER *DONE* 47 *TIMES IN A* ROW

* Attended class
* Ever had class
* Kept a chaw out of their cheek
* Dated the same sister
* Read this many words in a row without the aid of a dictionary

OKLAHOMA

been in charge of the Watergate investigation, Richard Nixon would still be president.

But the NCAA disagreed, and the Sooners got hit with a three-year probation and a one-year bowl game ban. Oh yeah, and I almost forgot—Coach Switzer was canned.

The boys in Norman laid low for a decade or two after that debacle, until 2006. Before that season, two players were asked to leave the team, including quarterback Rhett Bomar. Seems they had been working at a car dealership. Nothing wrong there, right? Well, when I say "working," I mean that they were collecting a paycheck but never actually showing up to work. Anyone who has ever watched *The Sopranos* knows how this works. The NCAA nicely asked OU to forfeit all their games from the 2005 season and to lose two scholarships for two years. OU sheepishly looked down and shuffled its feet around awhile before saying okay.

6

WE HATE NORMAN, EVERYONE NAMED NORMAN, AND ALL OKLAHOMA FANS

INFAMOUS SOONERS FANS

Music superstar Toby Keith loves him some Sooners football. Winner of such awards and titles as "Oklahoman of the Year" and "Entertainer of the Year," Keith enjoys watching OU play. He even sold cokes during games when he was a young boy. (Of course, all you have to do to qualify for Oklahoman of the Year is breathe through your nose for as long as it takes to forget your ABCs.)

Keith is, of course, a country singer. (What, you were expecting Pavarotti?) Despite his love of OU, his first hit, "Should've Been a Cowboy," is played by their rival, Oklahoma State.

Toby performed during the tribute to the late Oklahoma basketball great and jazz musician Wayman Tisdale. He also wrote the song "If You're Tryin' You Ain't" after a trainer said that at halftime during an OU game.

This Oklahoma native played defensive end in high school and also played for a semipro team. Keith is also a big fan of professional wrestling, which brings us to our next infamous fan.

"Stone Cold" Steve Austin is a former WWE wrestler and has been a big fan of the Sooners since Barry Switzer prowled the sideline in Norman. Austin spends most of his time these days working on his acting career. But we're not through talking about wrestling and infamous fans of OU football.

Say the name Edward McDaniel and some people may know who you're talking about. But say the name Wahoo McDaniel and you've got yourself a party—and possibly the most famous OU fan ever.

Wahoo was an Oklahoma football player during the late 1950s, and despite some trouble with missing a few classes and partying a little too much, he made his mark on the field as a kicker, fullback, and end. Born in 1938 in Bernice, Oklahoma, McDaniel was the son of Hugh "Big Wahoo" McDaniel. (In fact, Edward was actually called "Little Wahoo" in his youth.) He was of Chickasaw/Choctaw heritage, and proud of it.

Growing up in Midland, Texas, McDaniel became a fearsome running back during high school. He also had a baseball coach who would one day be more famous than himself—George H.W. Bush.

His hero was Jim Thorpe, so he became a star in the decathlon— that is until his fear of heights stopped him from trying the pole vault. (But no one made fun of him for his fear of heights.)

Once, on a bet, McDaniel ran from Norman to Chickasha—that's 10 more miles than a marathon. It took him six hours. Another bet had him eating a gallon jar of jalapeno peppers and drinking a quart of motor oil. The peppers didn't cause much of a fuss, but for weeks afterward, when he would sweat, he'd smell like a truck engine.

McDaniel became a linebacker and offensive guard for OU, and Coach Bud Wilkinson had his hands full. For every class Wahoo missed, he had to run the bleachers 25 times. By the time he left Norman, he had run up and down the stands 700 times. But he did have a talent for more than just trouble: he once punted a ball 91 yards. Only five other punts in college football history are longer.

McDaniel played linebacker for the Houston Oilers and then Denver before being traded to the New York Jets. The public address announcer at Shea Stadium had fun with his name. Whenever McDaniel would make a tackle—which happened quite often—the PA announcer would say, "Tackle by who?" And the fans would yell, "Wahoo!"

Miami chose him in the 1966 expansion draft, but his career with the Dolphins came to an end after he knocked out two police officers (the state sport in Oklahoma). He was traded to San Diego, but decided it was time for a career move. Wahoo took his brawling talents to an arena that appreciated them—pro wrestling—becoming famous throughout the South. He had already been rasslin' during the AFL off-seasons for extra cash. One of his signature moves was an overhead Tomahawk Chop.

He and Ric Flair began a feud that lasted for years and made both of them a lot of money. One memorable match had the two smashing a table at ringside, with Flair picking up a table leg and smacking Wahoo with it. Unbeknownst to Flair, the leg had a nail in it, and Wahoo was actually injured. Flair won the match and the title. But this wasn't much different from business as usual: Wahoo once estimated that he received 3,000 stitches during his career. Wahoo also wrestled against Abdullah the Butcher, Lex Luger, and Rowdy Roddy Piper.

In 1975 he was supposed to fly to an event with several other wrestlers, but at the last minute he decided to drive instead. The plane he was meant to be on crashed, injuring five wrestlers, including Flair and Johnny Valentine; Valentine's injuries were so severe that he was forced to retire. When Wahoo went to visit Flair in the hospital, the attendants at first thought he had come to finish a wrestling match.

To toughen himself up, Wahoo kept his house at 60°F. (In the Oklahoma tradition, whenever he felt a chill, he would throw another piece of sod on the fire.) Wahoo's partying ways were so legendary that he was mentioned in both Larry Csonka and Joe Namath's autobiographies. But he was also respected as an athlete. Super Bowl–winning quarterback Len Dawson of the Kansas City Chiefs says the hardest lick he ever took was from Wahoo.

McDaniel was inducted into the World Championship Wrestling Hall of Fame in 1995 along with the "Dean of Wrestling," Gordon Solie, and retired in 1996. He was inducted into the Professional Wrestling Hall of Fame in 2010.

Wahoo was married five times to four different women. Failing health resulted in the loss of both of his kidneys at the end of his life, and he was awaiting a transplant when he died in 2002.

SOONERS STUPID ENOUGH TO STUDY THERE

It's one thing to have the misfortune of being born in Oklahoma, but that's no excuse for going to college there, too.

Here are some of the more infamous "students" who spent their time incarcerated on the Norman campus.

Troy Aikman: Born in 1966 in West Covina, California, the former quarterback for the Dallas Cowboys won three Super Bowls and is a member of the Pro Football Hall of Fame. Aikman began his college career at OU before escaping to UCLA for some actual book-learnin'. Aikman went on to a successful career as a broadcaster after retiring from active play.

Carl Albert: Born in North McAlester, Oklahoma, in 1908, Albert was a congressman who served as Speaker of the U.S. House of Representatives from 1971 to 1977. He stood (and I use this term loosely) at 5'4". (Stand up and take a bow, Carl. Oh, you *are* standing.) Albert won a Rhodes Scholarship after attending OU. (They must have been holding lotteries for it back then.) He passed away in 2000.

Dick Armey: Born in 1940 in Cando, North Dakota, this fellow's name says it all. Well, that and he was a congressman from Texas. He earned a Ph.D. in economics from OU—which means he can balance his checkbook now.

Mookie Blaylock: Born in 1967 in Garland, Texas, Blaylock played basketball with the Atlanta Hawks and two other NBA teams. He played for Oklahoma, as well, and was known for his defense and passing skills. Oddly enough, famous grunge rockers Pearl Jam first went by the name "Mookie Blaylock."

Pat Bowlen: Born in 1944 in Prairie du Chien, Wisconsin, Bowlen is the owner of the NFL's Denver Broncos. He earned a degree in business from OU (yet was somehow still allowed to purchase the Broncos).

Sharon Clark: Born in 1943 in Seminole, Oklahoma, Clark was the *Playboy* Playmate of the Month for August 1970. At 27, she was the oldest woman ever to achieve that high office at that time. She was also an "actress." Clark studied sociology at OU. She told *Playboy* her goal was to teach English at a small university—I hear there's an opening at Oklahoma.

Bart Conner: Born in 1958 in Chicago, Illinois, Conner was a member of the gold medal–winning U.S. men's gymnastics team at the 1984 Los Angeles Olympics. He also won an individual gold medal on the parallel bars. Despite his amazing dexterity, somehow Connor could not extricate himself from attending OU. He is married to legendary Romanian gold medal–winning gymnast Nadia Comaneci, the first person to receive a perfect 10 score in the Olympic Games. Together they run the Bart Conner Gymnastics Academy in Norman. (So Comaneci escaped Romania for Oklahoma? You'd think you'd get a better reward for scoring a perfect 10.)

Larry Drake: Born in 1950 in Tulsa, Oklahoma, Drake is an actor best known for his Emmy Award–winning role on the television series *L.A. Law* and the film *Darkman*. Drake is a graduate of OU.

James Garner: Born in 1928 in Norman, Oklahoma, Garner is a well-known actor best known for lead roles in the television series *The Rockford Files* and *Maverick*. He also had roles in several movies. Garner's original last name was *Bumgarner*. Can't see why he would change that just for Hollywood. Maybe he was allowed to drop the *Bum* part when he left Okieville. Garner was the first person drafted out of Oklahoma during the Korean War and won two purple hearts while fighting there. He is a graduate of OU.

Alice Ghostley: Born in Eve, Missouri, in 1924, Ghostley was an actress best known for roles on the television series *Bewitched* and *Designing Women*. She also worked with fellow Okie James Garner on his western series *Nichols*. Ghostley attended OU before dropping out to pursue actors–uh, I mean acting. She passed away in 2007.

Blake Griffin: Born in 1989 in Oklahoma City, Oklahoma, Griffin became The Naismith College Player of the Year in basketball as a Sooner. He was drafted by and still plays for the NBA's Los Angeles Clippers and is known for his dunks. (He went from OU to the Clippers? Seems about right.)

Fred Haise: Born in 1933 in Biloxi, Mississippi, Haise was a NASA astronaut on the unfortunate Apollo 13 mission. He was supposed to be the sixth man to ever walk on the moon.

Haise is one of only 24 humans to ever fly to the moon. He earned a B.S. in aeronautical engineering with honors from OU in 1959.

Ed Harris: Born in 1950 in Englewood, New Jersey, Harris is an actor, director, and writer best known for movie roles in *Pollock, Radio, The Rock, The Abyss, The Truman Show,* and *Apollo 13,* in which his character helped save fellow Sooner and real-life astronaut Fred Haise. His father sang in the Fred Waring Chorus (Waring wrote the Sooners tune "OK Oklahoma"). He is married to actress Amy Madigan and studied drama at OU.

Van Heflin: Born in Walters, Oklahoma, in 1910, Heflin was an Oscar-winning actor who appeared in such films as *Johnny Eager, Airport, 3:10 to Yuma,* and *Shane.* He studied law at OU for two years before dropping out to sail the Pacific. (He preferred to face South Sea cannibals than stay in Oklahoma.) Heflin passed away in 1971.

Susan Kelly: Born in 1938 in Oklahoma, Kelly became the *Playboy* Playmate of the Month for May 1961. (Seems lots of OU women will pose nude in front of a camera in order to earn enough money to leave the state.) Kelly was also an "actress," and appeared on *The Joey Bishop Show* in 1962. Kelly earned a degree in education from OU (and also taught a lot of men about anatomy with her pictorial).

Anthony Kim: Born in 1985 in Los Angeles, California, Kim is a professional golfer. He studied and played golf at OU for three years and has three PGA Tour wins.

Shannon Lucid: Born in 1943 in Shanghai, China, Lucid was a NASA astronaut who once held the record for the longest stay in space by an American and by a woman. She has been in space five times. (Shows quite a desperate need to escape Oklahoma, allowing herself to be strapped inside a rocket and shot into orbit.) Lucid has a doctorate in biochemistry from OU (and uses it in a futile search for intelligent life in Oklahoma).

Larry Merchant: Born in 1931 in Brooklyn, New York, Merchant is a sportswriter and a boxing analyst for HBO. He is known for arguing with professional boxers—proof that he did indeed graduate from the University of Oklahoma.

Olivia Munn: Born in 1980 in Oklahoma City, Oklahoma, Munn is an actress (and some say a goddess). Best known for hosting the television show *Attack of the Show!* and costarring in *Perfect Couples*, a very funny show that NBC gave up on too soon. She is now a correspondent for *The Daily Show*. She also appeared in the film *Iron Man 2*. Munn is the best-looking human being to ever grace Soonerville, majoring in journalism with minors in Japanese and dramatic arts. I refuse to say anything bad about her in the hopes of one day meeting her.

Dari Nowkhah: Born in 1976 in Tulsa, Oklahoma, Nowkhah is a broadcaster on ESPN—and one of the few ESPN anchors whose head is neither larger than the screen or the sport they're covering. He earned a journalism degree from OU.

Tom Paxton: Born in 1937 in Chicago, Illinois, Paxton is a folk singer, songwriter, and strolling minstrel—in other words, a drain on society. He received a lifetime Grammy award (in return for agreeing to just go away and take that damn guitar with him). Paxton has written hundreds of songs (none of which you have ever heard, or will, unless you're kidnapped by aging hippies in a van) and majored in drama at OU.

Lance Rentzel: Born in 1943 in Flushing, New York, Rentzel was a running back at OU from 1962 to 1964 and a wide receiver from 1965 to 1974 on several NFL teams, including the Dallas Cowboys, the Minnesota Vikings, and the Los Angeles Rams. Longhorns fan and cycling legend Lance Armstrong is named after him. Armstrong might want to rethink that, since Rentzel was arrested in 1970 in Minnesota for exposing himself to a 10-year-old girl. His wife at the time, entertainer Joey Heatherton, divorced him after that incident. If you've ever seen how beautiful she was back in the day, you know how stupid he was to blow that relationship.

Joe Simpson: Born in 1951 in Purcell, Oklahoma, Simpson is a former major league ballplayer for the Los Angeles Dodgers, the Seattle Mariners, and the Kansas City Royals. He was an All-America outfielder and first baseman at OU. Since retiring from the playing field, Simpson has become a broadcaster for the Atlanta Braves. (Must seem like heaven after Oklahoma.)

Wayman Tisdale: Born in Fort Worth, Texas, in 1964, Tisdale played basketball for OU and was inducted into the National Collegiate Basketball Hall of Fame in 2009. He was an NBA player who later became a well-respected jazz bass guitarist after retiring from the game. Tisdale passed away in 2009.

Dennis Weaver: Born in 1924 in Joplin, Missouri, Weaver was an actor best known for the lead role in the television series *McCloud*. He also appeared on *Gunsmoke* and starred in the TV movie *Duel*, the first film directed by Steven Spielberg. Weaver was a navy pilot during World War II and studied drama at OU, where he also starred in track. Weaver passed away in 2006.

THE TOUCHDOWN CLUB

The Touchdown Club supports the OU football team, a tradition begun in 1947. Some of the events sponsored by the club include the Fall Kickoff Dinner Meeting, the Spring Football Lunch Meeting, and the Annual OU-TX Brunch, which is held in Dallas. They are also in charge of making sure the potato salad isn't left out in the sun for too long.

Over the decades, the Touchdown Club has raised more than $6 million dollars to help fund scholarships and other athletic department needs (including bail money and fees for attorneys).

If you like the look of the turf at Owen Field, you can thank the Touchdown Club, since they've been upgrading it for over 30 seasons. The grass is so well maintained that the cheerleaders graze on it. Refurbishing practice facilities and weight rooms are also on their agenda; they make sure the team is well-stocked with dumbbells (a responsibility shared by the recruiting staff).

NORMAN, OKLAHOMA

The relationship between the city of Norman and the University of Oklahoma is one beneficial to both—they work together like a proctologist's hand in a glove.

Money Magazine calls Norman one of the top 10 towns in America. They also call the stimulus package a huge success. Amazingly, they point out the location of the school as one of the main reasons Norman ranks so high. Those editors really need to get out of Manhattan now and then. No other Big 12 city was even in the top 50. Now *that* I can believe.

Norman is a place to come and study, then stay and raise a family and start a business. (If you like studying agrarian issues, raising children in barns, and working with swine.) Homes are affordable in Norman—even those without wheels—and if the football team isn't playing, you can check out the Fred Jones Jr. Museum on campus, which houses the classic works of such luminaries as Monet, Renoir, and Degas. It holds the largest gift of French Impressionist paintings ever donated to a college. Why? Because the previous owner mistakenly thought he was giving them to Norman *Rockwell*.

Named after a young surveyor who had his name scratched into an elm tree as a prank in 1870, Norman has grown into the third-largest city in Oklahoma with 107,000 people—the majority of whom now own shoes.

As for the university, it has grown from 100 students in 1895 to more than 31,000 today (the majority of whom do not yet own shoes). Amazingly, only Harvard has more Rhodes Scholars among its graduates. Talk about pearls before swine.

STUPID PLAYER NICKNAMES

Tackle Gilford Duggan was an All-American in 1939, and the year before he was part of a defense that allowed a measly 43 yards per game. Duggan was drafted by the Giants in 1940, but he lives forever in Sooners lore because of his nickname, "Cactus Face."

End Frank "Pop" Ivy was part of the legendary 1938 Sooners defense that allowed only two touchdowns during the regular season. Grantland Rice, the most famous sportswriter of his day, said that Ivy was one of the greatest defensive ends he'd ever seen. "Pop" got his nickname due to premature baldness.

Ivy would later win three Grey Cups as head coach of the Edmonton Eskimos of the CFL. He was also the head coach of the NFL Chicago Cardinals and AFL Houston Oilers (but not at the same time).

A lifelong resident of Oklahoma, Ivy once quit a job as an assistant coach with the New York Giants because he didn't want to live in the New York/New Jersey area during the off-season—so he must have had some sense.

Tackle Roy "Soupy" Smoot was a bowling ball of a man, but his shape helped to hide blazing speed for a man his size. Smoot was so quick that in 1919, he blocked not one but two punts before the ball ever left the punter's foot. He was the first lineman in Oklahoma history to be an All-American.

Two-time All-American halfback and defensive back Tommy "Shoo-Fly" McDonald could also throw a mean pass when called upon. He won Player of the Year with the Maxwell Award in 1956, and the *Sporting News* Award, too. In 1955 he became the first Oklahoma player to score a touchdown in every game of one season.

McDonald was drafted by the Eagles in 1957 and entered the Pro Football Hall of Fame in 1998. He was also inducted into the National Football Foundation College Football Hall of Fame in 1985. He is the shortest player ever inducted into Canton.

McDonald's talents didn't end at the sideline. He was also an exceptional portrait painter—the Toulouse Lautrec of football, if you will.

Fullback Forest "Spot" Geyer was captain of the 10–0 team of 1915, which set a school mark for the best record up to that time. He was known for an exceptionally strong and accurate arm, hence his nickname. (It wasn't just because he smelled like a wet dog.) Geyer was also a kicker and was inducted into the National Football Foundation College Football Hall of Fame in 1973. Spot was also a pointer.

STUPIDER SOONERS STORIES

The very first game acknowledged by the university (and the parole board) was all the way back in 1895, when Oklahoma wasn't even a state and wouldn't be one for 12 more years. The school itself was barely three years old at the time—perfect for its intellectual level.

It was a one-game season, and a losing one, under head coach John A. Harts, who lost his only turn on the field 34–0 in Oklahoma City. It was a rough-and-tumble game with so many injuries that Oklahoma had to borrow some players from the town team in order to finish the contest. (These recruits included old women and a one-eyed dog.)

The taste of defeat did not sit well with the Sooners, a problem quickly remedied the next year under new coach Vernon Louis Parrington. The schedule was doubled that year, and OU took both games over some stiff competition—Norman High School. (Hey, a win is a win, and a lot of colleges were playing town teams and high schools in the early days. Women's colleges, that is.) After their opening loss in November 1895, OU didn't lose again until nearly the next century, falling to Arkansas City in November of 1899.

The first victory over another *college* team occurred on December 31, 1897, with a 17–8 win over Kingfisher College in Guthrie. It would be the beginning of a long string of spankings of tiny Kingfisher, which became so disheartened that in 1927, they decided to live the old adage "If you can't beat 'em, join 'em" by letting themselves be absorbed by OU.

Oklahoma never lost to Kingfisher in 22 games. The best the other team could muster were three lousy ties. During one 10-year stretch, Kingfisher would only score 17 points. It was like pounding on your little brother, if your little brother was only five-years-old. And sickly.

But a great story came out of that first matchup, as most of the spectators had never seen a football game before. One of them was the Logan County Sheriff, who upon first arriving at the scene thought a drunken brawl had broken out. And he might have been right, since he discovered one of the Kingfisher players had hidden a stovepipe up his sleeve. This addition to the uniform was not thought to be conducive to good sportsmanship, but considering the one-sided history of this series, it was perfectly understandable.

The Oklahoma boys loved playing the Arkansas City, Kansas, town team because it meant they could stay in a hotel with an accommodating pleasure not seen much at the time in Oklahoma: a bathtub.

In 1898 OU made their first road trip outside Oklahoma to play in Arkansas City. As you would expect from Okies, not all the players were seasoned world-travelers at the time—especially a young man by the name of Tom Tribbey. Sooners historian Harold Keith wrote about Tribbey's first train ride:

> Green as the corn on his father's Pottawatomie County farm and only eighteen years old, Tribbey came to the university to study pharmacy. He had never ridden on a train until the team loaded him on the north-bound Santa Fe for the Arkansas City game. When the cars began to leave the station, Tribbey gasped with wonder, clutched the guards of the green plush seat in which he was sitting and blurted out delightedly, "Gosh, fellers! She's a movin'!"

It was a phrase he would also utter on his wedding night.

The first win over a state university (and a college team that the civilized world might have actually heard of) occurred in

October 1899, with an 11–5 victory over Arkansas in Shawnee. The Oklahoma team was not known as the Sooners in those days, but instead called themselves the Rough Riders, the name made famous by the First U.S. Volunteer Cavalry Unit led by Theodore Roosevelt during the Spanish-American War. Several hundred Oklahomans rallied around the war effort and volunteered for the unit.

Coach Parrington would step down as head coach after the 1900 season, but would stay with the school and later win the Pulitzer Prize for history in 1928. (Which explains why he had to step down as their football coach—he was much too intelligent.)

That year also saw the beginning of Oklahoma's greatest rivalry, against the University of Texas at Austin. There's a whole chapter of this book dedicated to that hallowed series.

In 1904 OU destroyed Oklahoma A&M 75–0; that school would later be known and reviled as Oklahoma State. The game was held in Guthrie, and every player on the OU team scored a touchdown. Cowboys? More like Cowgirls.

You'd think a shellacking like that would be what most people would remember from that contest, but the strange story of Ed Cook was actually more memorable. Seems Cook had to swim out into Cottonwood Creek to retrieve a wayward football before he could score his touchdown. The Aggie punter kicked the ball into such a stiff wind that it carried the football backward into the rain-swollen creek. Despite a natural aversion to water, Cook dived into the cold stream and beat all the others to the ball, swimming with it to the opposite bank and touching it to the ground for the score. (That made him the first OU player ever to have a bath before, during, or after a game.)

Coach Fred Ewing would leave the team after the 1904 season, but he also managed to leave a little legacy. Ewing began taping the ankles of his players with adhesive bandages to protect against sprains, something he started long before other teams picked up the habit. Accordingly, Ewing left to return to medical school.

The Bedlam Series is the annual game against in-state "rival" Oklahoma State. Dictionary.com defines *rivalry* as "The state or condition of competition or antagonism." The antagonism is there between OU and OSU, but competition? Not really, not when you realize that the Sooners have won 82 out of the 106 games the two teams have played. Doesn't one side have to win every now and then to make a series a rivalry? That first game held in 1904 in Guthrie was the one that featured Oklahoma's Ed Cook recovering that punt from a creek for a touchdown. It was plays like that which led spectators to describe the 75–0 OU win as *bedlam*—and thus a name was born.

A recent book made an accusation that the 1954 Bedlam game was fixed by mobsters. The legend goes that a cook was bribed to place laxatives in soup eaten by Oklahoma's players, making them very ill in the days leading up to the game. That certainly would bring new meaning to the term *running game*.

The Sooners managed to win anyway, 14–0, but they didn't win by the 20 points the spread dictated. Most people still around to remember that contest don't recall events playing out quite that way, however, and those in the know consider the story to be a bit of a fiction.

It's very fitting that the final Big 12 title game in 2010 was between Oklahoma and Nebraska. It's even more fitting that No. 10 OU rallied from a 17–0 deficit for a 23–20 victory over the No. 13 Cornhuskers. The two teams have met more than 80 times, but this may be it for a while, since Nebraska took its ball to the Big 10.

These two dynamos ruled the Big 8 for decades, and each has had its share of success in the Big 12, with the lion's share going to the Sooners.

Before 2010, the two teams had only met once in the Big 12 title tilt. It was December 2, 2006, in Kansas City's Arrowhead Stadium, and Oklahoma won easily, 21–7. Jermaine Gresham's catch of a Paul Thompson pass was the big blow.

Before then, you had to go all the way back to the Big 8 championship game of November 19, 1988, held at Norman, to find a contest between these two that had a title on the line. Neither team had lost in conference play that season. This close game went to Nebraska, 7–3. The loss was doubly hurtful for the Sooners; they lost their quarterback, Charles Thompson, to a broken leg, and head coach Barry Switzer's knee was taken out when a player collided with him on the sideline. (Too bad it didn't hurt him in a less-essential spot— like, say, his head.)

EVEN STUPIDER SOONERS LAWS

★ If you're a promoter and were planning on promoting a "horse tripping" event—whatever that is—in the state of Oklahoma, you're out of luck, because it's illegal.

★ Do not get caught by the authorities holding a fish in a fishbowl while riding on a public bus in Norman. I suppose they prefer you to carry them in your pocket.

★ It is illegal for bar owners to allow their patrons to simulate having sex with a buffalo in Norman. Bison beware, however—outside of the bar seems to be fair game.

★ You must be licensed by the state of Oklahoma before you can do *your own* hair. But that only goes for the ladies—you male Sooners are free to coif it up.

★ It is against the law to wear boots to bed in Oklahoma. No mention is made of spurs.

★ It is illegal to take a bite out of another person's hamburger in Oklahoma. (Wimpy, that goes for you, too.)

★ Tattoos were banned in Oklahoma until the law was repealed in 2006. The last Oklahoman not in jail signed the repeal into law.

★ You may not drive a car whilst reading a comic book in Oklahoma. This law is focused on the three Okies who can read.

★ Whaling is illegal in Oklahoma. For the geographically challenged, I will repeat that: whaling is illegal in *land-locked* Oklahoma. (This law was put in place to protect the OU cheerleaders.)

★ Those who find it amusing to make "ugly faces" at dogs in Oklahoma run the risk of a fine or jail time.

★ Also in this great state, it is against the law to have the hind legs of a farm animal in your boots—especially while they are still attached to the farm animal. ("Honestly officer, I was just helping this sheep over the fence.")

★ Dogs must have a signed document from the mayor of Norman allowing them to congregate in groups of more than three on private property. (Groups of three or more are allowed to congregate on public grounds in order to hold their anti-dog-congregation-law rallies.)

★ If you are caught wearing New York Jets gear in Ada, Oklahoma, you face incarceration. (Actually, I kind of agree with this law.)

★ In Yukon, Oklahoma, you must honk your horn when passing another vehicle. Yukon is known as "The World's Loudest Backwater." They are very proud of this moniker.

★ In Bartlesville, you may not own more than two adult cats at one time. However, you may turn your home into a lemur habitat for all the town cares. It is also illegal to make "annoying vibrations." Somehow this has to have something to do with the law concerning cats.

★ In Wynona, you may not wash your—or anyone else's—clothes in a bird bath. It's perfectly legal in Naomi, however. Bird baths must be held in special esteem in Wynona, seeing is how it's also illegal to allow your mule to drink from them.

★ In Hawthorne, it is illegal to place hypnotized people in display windows. Everyone knows they belong in the bird bath.

★ In Tulsa, elephants are not welcome downtown. If you have any questions, please see "The Great Stampede of 1898" exhibit at the town hall.

★ In Oklahoma City, the mayor may not go on strike—even if the populace wishes him or her to do so. Also, don't even think about walking backward downtown while eating a hamburger. (Once again, Wimpy, this goes for you, too.)

★ In Schulter, ladies may not gamble while wearing a towel, lingerie, or nothing at all. If they look anything like most women from Oklahoma, this is perfectly understandable. (With the exception of my friend Karla Meinberg, formerly of El Reno, Oklahoma.)

ABOUT THE AUTHOR

BORN IN HOUSTON, Mississippi, Pete Davis lives in Atlanta and has an enormous love of college football. He has lived throughout the South, including Arkansas, Alabama, and Virginia. He delayed college for three years by surfing in San Diego. Close ties to both Texas and Oklahoma have made the writing of this book very enjoyable.

After receiving a degree in broadcast journalism from Georgia State University (which now has its own football team, thank you very much) he spent 20 years in radio as a talk show host, sports director, writer, producer, reporter, and anchor. Pete was the sideline reporter for the Atlanta Falcons broadcasts for five seasons, including their Super Bowl game against the Denver Broncos in Miami.

He is the winner of four Associated Press awards, including the 2003 Georgia Associated Press Broadcaster Association Award for Best Sports Program and the 2001 Georgia AP Broadcaster Association Award for Best Sports Play-by-Play.

Pete has been cohost for UPN-TV coverage of the Jerry Lewis Telethon for the Muscular Dystrophy Association and, besides this book, has written a novel and two plays, which can be found on Amazon.com's Kindle.

He grew up wanting to be either an option quarterback in the wishbone offense or Archie Manning.

tongue to give the most bizarre yet effective pep talk in Texas history:

> Men, we will have to face the fact that our coach is incompetent. It is true that he should be taking lessons from us, rather than we from him. But the fact remains that he is employed to handle the team and is certainly the head of the football organization. I want to earnestly urge you to keep your mouths shut and follow the directions of the coach every day you are on the field. If you are instructed to do something that you know to be bad football, do the thing willingly and promptly at the time and then come to me about it. I will see that all mistakes are remedied.

If only we had a man like Parrish in Washington, D.C., today.

Despite finishing 9–1, Schenker's contract was not renewed, which made him the second Longhorns coach to be fired after losing only one game. This led to Texas hiring W.E. Metzenthin, a German professor at the university and a native of that country. He actually led them to winning records in both seasons he coached. Metzenthin probably looked upon every opponent as France. But he retired shortly thereafter because he was tired of being criticized by the fans. And this was before blogging.

WILLIAM S. "BILLY" WASMUND AND DAVE ALLERDICE

The strangest era in Longhorns football was about to begin. In 1910 the school decided to stop hiring coaches from Eastern schools, picking one from the Midwest instead. William S. "Billy" Wasmund came from Michigan with a belief in

strength training and conditioning. Accordingly, for their second season under Wasmund, the boys were in prime shape and ready to roll. Unfortunately, Wasmund would not be there with them.

Just six days before the season opener against the Horned Frogs, Wasmund was found unconscious near his second-floor apartment. At first police thought that foul play was involved, but it was soon discovered that the known sleepwalker had actually plunged from his balcony during the night. Wasmund rallied, and for a time his prognosis looked good, but he took a turn for the worse and died a few days later. (It was the first time a coach had ever literally been bounced from the job.) The game with TCU was canceled.

But even a deadly fall couldn't stop Wasmund from helping his team. On his deathbed he had recommended his former Wolverines teammate Dave Allerdice to replace him. It was a sage endorsement. Allerdice was a calming influence in those troubled times, and became the most successful coach in Longhorns history up to that point.

Allerdice's tenure included a 92–0 thrashing of Daniel Baker, which is still the largest margin of victory and most points scored by a UT team. They also joined the Southwest Conference during Allerdice's time with the team. During their first season in the SWC, he also led the Longhorns to a 6–3 record. They were 33–7 overall during his time as coach.

But Allerdice abruptly resigned after the 1915 season, citing the "super critical nature of the Texas fans" as his reason— becoming the third Longhorns coach to name that as the

cause of his departure. He moved back to his hometown of Indianapolis and there entered the family meat packing business, where once again he was in charge of steers.

Unfortunately, just like his friend and predecessor Wasmund, Allerdice would die tragically. He and his family perished in a house fire during Christmas of 1940.

He entered the Longhorn Hall of Honor in 1981.

BILL JUNEAU, BERRY M. WHITAKER, AND E.J. STEWART

Bill Juneau was the next coach to leave because of pressure to win, even though he had a 19–7 record. But not winning an SWC crown during the first five seasons of the conference proved his undoing. He left for Alaska, where he lobbied to have the capital city named after him—but locals decided to name it after gold prospector Joe Juneau instead. Okay, I'm making that part up—but Juneau did go to Alaska.

The unceasing pressure to win was also too much for Juneau's successor, a man by the name of Berry M. Whitaker. He had plenty of offers, but came to Texas for a strange reason— Austin was the offer located the furthest from his hometown of Anderson, Indiana. History has made no record of what that town ever did to him.

Coach Whitaker posted a sterling 22–3–1 record, but found the work so stressful that he developed ulcers and decided to quit while he was still ahead. He was inducted into the Longhorn Hall of Honor in 1977.

The next coach didn't quit, but probably wished he had. E.J. Stewart had a 24–9–3 record, but was fired for not winning enough, suffering the same fate as many of his predecessors.

And fate wasn't through with Stewart. Tragedy struck again, as it had with Coaches Wasmund and Allerdice. Just three years after he left UT, Stewart was shot and killed by a fellow deer hunter.

And no, it was not Dick Cheney.

CLYDE LITTLEFIELD and JACK CHEVIGNY

If ever there was an example of how important the tradition of winning is at the University of Texas, it comes with the story of Coach Clyde Littlefield.

Clyde was a legendary player in several sports for the Longhorns before becoming head coach of the football team in 1927. He became the first Longhorns coach to win two SWC titles, amassing an impressive 44–18–6 record along the way.

But the 1933 team went 4–5–2, becoming the first team to have a losing campaign in the 40-plus year history of football at the school. Powerful forces around the school wanted him fired, yet he also had many supporters. Littlefield, however, abhorred the politics and so decided to resign. He entered the Longhorn Hall of Honor in 1961.

Littlefield's replacement had a fast rise and an even faster fall. But his story is such a one for the ages that even Forrest Gump would be proud of him.

Jack Chevigny was known throughout the country before even arriving in Austin. He played for Knute Rockne at Notre Dame and scored a touchdown against Army after the coach's famous "Win one for the Gipper" halftime speech. Legend has it that Chevigny actually said, "That's one for the Gipper," as he crossed the goal line.

Some say Chevigny was being groomed to replace Rockne when the great man retired, but the coach died in a plane crash before Chevigny was ready to take his place. After a stint coaching the NFL Chicago Cardinals, Chevigny became the Longhorns head coach and started off strong, but wins became harder to come by, and he resigned with the first and only losing record ever for a UT coach, 13–14–2.

Chevigny had a tragic but heroic end. He became a first lieutenant in the Marines during World War II and was killed during the Battle of Iwo Jima. And this is where the story gets weird. Some say this is only a tall tale, but it's been repeated enough times to enter UT lore. During his first season as coach at UT, he led them to a huge 7–6 upset of the Fighting Irish. The coach was presented with a pen inscribed with the words "To a Notre Dame boy who beat Notre Dame." Eleven years later Chevigny was among the first waves of Marines to hit the beaches of Iwo Jima. Some say he was killed by a sniper and some say it was a direct hit by a shell. But six months later, in September of 1945, the war was over and the battleship *U.S.S. Missouri* entered Tokyo Bay for the signing of the peace treaty with the empire of Japan. As the Japanese envoy was about to sign, an American noticed the envoy's pen had English words inscribed on it. It was the same pen given to Jack Chevigny in 1934!

Somehow, against all odds, the pen had been found on the island by Japanese soldiers and had worked its way back to the mainland to find itself the focal point of history.

Losing record? I think not.

DANA X. BIBLE, BLAIR CHERRY, AND ED PRICE

The Bible is known as the good book, and Dana X. Bible was known as a good coach when he arrived in Austin. When he left coaching 10 years later, he was the best coach Texas had ever had up until that time.

Bible had already led successful programs at Texas A&M and Nebraska before coming to Texas. In fact, his services were in such demand that at one point he was both an assistant coach at A&M and LSU at the same time!

But he got off to a rocky start with the Longhorns, winning only three games during his first two seasons. The fans had the patience of Job with Dana—maybe the *Bible* name gave them pause—and they were duly rewarded, with 63 victories and three SWC championships.

Bible's 1942 team was the first UT squad to play in a bowl game, beating Georgia Tech 14–7 in the Cotton Bowl. When he retired, his 198 victories were surpassed by only two legends, Amos Alonzo Stagg and Pop Warner.

But it took Bible only 33 years to amass such a total, while it took Stagg 57 seasons and Warner 44 to accomplish their

feats. And Bible never lost a bowl game, going 2–0–1 in three Cotton Bowls.

He entered the College Football Hall of Fame in 1951 and the Longhorn Hall of Honor in 1960.

Blair Cherry was literally cherry-picked by Bible as his successor, and succeed he did.

Dana X. Bible amassed 198 victories in his 33 years as head coach of the Longhorns. Here he watches from the sideline during the Texas A&M game in 1946, his last season as coach before becoming Texas' athletics director.

Cherry was 32–10–1, and was so successful that both the Chicago Cardinals and the Washington Redskins tried to lure him away to the NFL. But he chose to remain in Austin. Maybe if he had gone to the pros, he might have avoided the pressure of being the coach at Texas, which ultimately led to him developing ulcers and insomnia to the point that midway through the great season of 1950, he announced that he was retiring in order to enter the oil business at the end of the year.

A year later he wrote an article for a national publication, stating that the "over-emphasis on winning" at UT, combined with critical media and fan pressure, had been too much for him.

He made the Longhorn Hall of Honor in 1968.

Ed Price was next, winning two conference titles during his first three seasons, but a 1–9 debacle in 1956 was his undoing. It was the worst season in Longhorns history and led to his resignation.

He entered the Longhorn Hall of Honor in 1967.

DARRELL ROYAL

Price's departure set the stage for the greatest coach in Texas Longhorns history. Athletics Director Dana Bible's legacy continued to shine when he hired former Oklahoma star Darrell Royal.

Royal had been head coach with the Edmonton Eskimos of the Canadian Football League, Mississippi State, and the Washington Huskies before coming to Austin.

DARRELL ROYAL
QUOTES WE LOVE

"The good news is there're 17 million people who care about Texas football. The bad news is there're 17 million people who care about Texas football."

"If worms carried pistols, birds wouldn't eat 'em."

"You've got to think lucky. If you fall into a mud hole, check your back pocket: you might have caught a fish."

"Breaks balance out. The sun don't shine on the same ole dog's rear end every day."

"Sometimes you have to suck it up and call a number."

"Punt returns will kill you quicker than a minnow can swim a dipper."

"He's not very fast, but maybe Elizabeth Taylor can't sing."

"Football doesn't build character. It eliminates the weak ones."

"You never lose a game if the opponent doesn't score."

"I learned this about coaching: you don't have to explain victory and you can't explain defeat."

Over the next glorious 20 years, he never had a losing season, leading the Longhorns to their first national title in 1963, then

to two others in 1969 and 1970. Overall, he was 167–47–5 at Texas, with a league-record 11 Southwest Conference championships. And it was Royal's gift for leadership that allowed offensive genius Emory Bellard to invent the wishbone offense in 1968, a development that revolutionized both the Longhorns and college football.

Royal's teams were virtually unbeatable at home, winning 42 consecutive games at one point. They won the SWC for six straight years, and for six straight years they enjoyed playing in the Cotton Bowl. Twenty-six All-Americans took the field under Royal.

FRED AKERS

There were humongous shoes to fill when Royal retired in 1976. A former assistant coach, Fred Akers, was the man to try them on. Royal had wanted longtime assistant Mike Campbell to get the job, but Akers' success as a head coach at Wyoming swayed the decision.

Akers took one look at running back Earl Campbell and decided the "I" formation was the best route to follow. That was a wise decision, obviously, since it led to a Heisman Trophy. Akers went 11–0 during his first regular season and seemed poised to win the national title, but a 38–10 loss to Notre Dame in the Cotton Bowl ended those hopes.

Akers went on to amass the second-most wins as a Longhorns coach at the time (only Royal had more), going 86–31–2 in 10 seasons. But his two SWC titles were not enough to hold off the wolves that began circling when recruiting violations

started piling up and losses became more frequent. He was let go in 1986.

David McWilliams and John Mackovic were the next two coaches. They both enjoyed moderate success, but not up to the standards Texas fans expected. It would be up to a man named Mack to bring the program back to the top.

MACK BROWN

Mack Brown arrived in Austin in 1998 after turning around the program at North Carolina. He immediately led the Longhorns to a 9–3 record and a berth in the Cotton Bowl.

Since then he's taken UT to two more Cotton Bowls, five Holiday Bowls, an Alamo Bowl, a Fiesta Bowl, and three Rose Bowls, including the one in which he won the National Championship in 2006. His teams were the first at UT to win five bowl games in a row. In fact, he's taken Texas to a bowl game during every year of his tenure except one.

Brown has a .783 winning percentage with a record of 141–39, including a stretch of nine straight seasons with double digit wins, the second-longest such streak in NCAA history.

Brown was honored with the Bobby Dodd National Coach of the Year award in 2008 and was named Big 12 Coach of the Year in 2009. In 2005 he was named the Paul W. "Bear" Bryant National Coach of the Year.

Only he and Darrell Royal have won more than 100 games at Texas, which is why Brown is already in the Longhorn Hall of Honor. He and Royal have a close working relationship.

Brown is also known for his sense of humor, especially when he appeared in commercials for ESPN's *GameDay* show. In one, Brown played the game Jenga with Alabama coach Nick Saban, and in another he chastised color analyst Kirk Herbstreit for changing the lyrics of "Texas Fight," saying, "We don't free-style 'Texas Fight,' big boy."

MACK BROWN QUOTES WE LOVE

"You don't belong in a game like this if you don't feel good about yourself and walk with a swagger. If you think you can be stopped, this isn't the place for you."

"When you become No. 1 and everybody talks about how much you're going to kill the other team, and they've done nothing but lose, and you're on the road, and it's at night, and it's cold, it's a trap game."

5

WE LOVE TEXAS TRADITION

MAGNIFICENT MASCOT

Bevo is his name.

He's a Longhorn steer, and there's no controversy when it comes to him being one of the grandest and most impressive mascots in college football. And maybe the one you'd least want to mess with this side of Mike the Tiger at LSU—although you *can* get your picture taken with him at the games in Austin. Don't worry. There are two handlers there to make sure he behaves.

But there is some controversy as to how he got his name; in fact, there are at least three versions of the story, involving, among other things, branding, barbecues, beer breweries, kidnapping, and cattle rustling. This mascot has it all, including an origin story worthy of James Bond by way of Louis L'Amour.

It all started back in the year 1916 in Austin on Thanksgiving Day. The Longhorns were at home against visiting Texas A&M, which in those days was known as the A&M College of Texas. But no matter what they called themselves, the Aggies were still a pain to UT fans.

The game was tied 7–7 at halftime when suddenly a half-starved, bright orange Longhorn steer was dragged out onto the field and presented to the student body by a group of alumni known as the Texas Exes. They were led by Stephen Pinckney, class of 1911, who had a dream to find a living mascot for the school.

And find one he did, under strange circumstances—battling cattle rustlers in West Texas while working for the U.S. attorney general's office. A raid near Laredo produced a steer whose coat was so orange that it lit up Pinckney's eyes. He'd found his man—or steer, that is. Asking for just a dollar each from 124 fellow alumni, Pinckney purchased the purloined pet and promptly packed him on a train to Austin.

He only forgot two things: food and water. Not surprisingly, this long-suffering Longhorn arrived in a very foul mood just in time for the game.

After the on-field presentation, the steer was taken to a South Austin stockyard for a long overdue meal and an official photograph. Unfortunately, the photo took place before the feeding, and the flash bulb startled the bad-tempered bovine into charging the cameraman, who barely escaped the pen with his life and camera intact.

I know that none of this has anything to do with the name *Bevo*. Patience—we're getting to that part.

Meanwhile, back at the game, the Horns ran back two punts for touchdowns and won the game easily, 21–7. This did not sit

well with the Aggies, so they bided their time and made their plans for revenge.

In the next month's edition of the Texas Exes magazine, called *Alcalde*, editor Ben Dyer was the first to name the new mascot in print, writing, "His name is Bevo. Long may he reign!"

Bevo, the University of Texas mascot, stands in the north end zone before the start of the 2006 Texas-Oklahoma game at the Cotton Bowl.

So now the moniker was official—but where did it come from?

The story goes that when the football season was over, Bevo was living large down in South Austin. What to do with him was quite the debate around campus. Some wanted to brand a huge *T* on one side and *21–7* on the other as a reminder of the win. But even in 1916, most people considered that rather cruel, and wondered if just maybe the animal could be tamed enough for it to roam freely around campus, grazing on the Forty Acres.

That debate came to an end early Sunday morning on February 12, 1917. That's when four brigands from A&M broke into the stockyard with all the utensils needed for steer branding.

Bevo struggled mightily, but they finally managed to burn *13–0*—the final score of the Aggies' win over UT two years before at College Station—into his hide.

This dastardly act caused much concern and consternation, to the point that rumors began to swirl that the Aggies were not through and the mascot was in further danger. This led to him being moved to a safe ranch 60 miles west of Austin. Sadly, this was the beginning of the end for the first Bevo.

Shortly after that time, America's involvement in World War I began, and Bevo was largely forgotten until 1919, when the school remembered it was paying 50¢ a day for his room and board. Unfortunately, Bevo was no closer to being tamed, so the idea of letting him wander free around the campus and football field was tabled. And so was Bevo, for that matter.

PETA members may want to look away at this point. For sadly, Bevo was fattened up and made the guest of honor, so to speak, as the barbecued main dish for the January 1920 football banquet. Ironically, and strangely, the Aggies were invited to dine on their former nemesis. They were served the side of Bevo beef that they had branded, and were also given the hide with the *13–0* brand on it.

A&M fans have always claimed that they were the inspiration for Bevo's name. The story goes that the *13–0* was changed by Texas branders, who turned the *13* into a *B*, the dash into an *E*, and added a *V* between the *E* and the zero, thus forming the letters *B-E-V-O*.

While this all makes for a great story, the *Alcalde* magazine article actually came out two months before the initial branding took place.

Some say the name came from a popular soft drink at the time called Bevo, which was produced by the Anheuser-Busch brewery up in St. Louis as an antidote to Prohibition's ban on alcohol. The product name Bevo was a play on the Bohemian word for beer, which is *pivo*. But debunking that theory is fairly simple, since that near-beer product was not well known around Austin at that time.

So where exactly *did* the name come from? A 1993 graduate of UT may hold the real answer. Dan Zabcik thinks the name came from a popular cartoon strip found in national and local newspapers at the time. Written by Gus Mager, the strip featured monkeys with various names that all ending

with the letter O. The strip was so popular that it's even credited by some as the inspiration for the Marx Brothers' names (Groucho, Chico, Harpo, and Zeppo).

Zabcik thinks the word *beevo*, which is plural for beef, was just shortened by one letter to form Bevo. *Beeve* is also a slang term used to describe a cow that's about to be eaten, which, sadly for Bevo, was all too accurate.

So the facts seem to point to one conclusion: Bevo got his name from Longhorns fans and not Aggies.

But don't tell that to nationally syndicated radio host Neal Boortz. The proud Texas A&M graduate is known for telling stories concerning his days matriculating in College Station, including the tale about the Aggies kidnapping Bevo and surreptitiously serving him up to unsuspecting UT fans as a pregame tailgate meal, with the question "How're your steaks?" leading to much merriment for the A&M crowd.

Whether those stories are true or not, Bevo is still a great tradition and an interesting part of Longhorns Lore.

Unless you're Bevo, that is.

PIG THE DOG

Just about everyone knows that the official mascot of UT is Bevo the Longhorn steer. But before Bevo there was a dog mascot. A dog named Pig. Pig the Dog. Actually, his full name was Pig Bellmont.

In 1914, at the young age of just seven weeks, a small, white and tan pit bull mix was brought to campus by Theo Bellmont, the school's first athletics director.

Around that same time, Texas had a player named Gus "Pig" Dittmar. It was Dittmar who loaned his nickname to Texas' first mascot. Dittmar had gained the moniker "Pig" because he slipped through defensive lines like a greased pig. During one game, Dittmar was standing on the sideline next to the dog when someone noticed that they had bowlegs. And thus, Pig the Dog was given his name.

Pig's sty, or home, was the entire campus. He even slept on the steps of the University Co-op and was known as the Varsity Mascot.

Pig attended classes, ballgames both home and away, and was known to snarl whenever the subject of Texas A&M was broached. During World War I, when the campus hosted air cadets, Pig would join them every morning when they gathered.

On cold days you could find Pig, like any good student, lounging in the warm library. He was even declared an official University of Texas letterman and sported a brass T on his collar.

But Pig's run came to an end, literally and sadly, on New Year's Day in 1923. He was accidentally hit by a Model T at the corner of Guadalupe and 24th Streets in Austin. Being Texas tough, Pig initially shook off the collision, walking it off and seeming only slightly hurt. But his body was found a few days later.

Pig lay in state in front of the Co-op in a coffin draped in orange and white ribbons. Mourners by the hundreds paid their respects with tips of the hat and sniffles. A funeral procession led by the Longhorn Band brought his body to a spot on campus under a grove of oak trees, where Pig was laid to rest.

The Dean of the School of Engineering, Dr. Thomas Taylor, delivered the serious eulogy. Dr. Thomas said Pig would take his place among the great dogs of the earth. A lone trumpeter played "Taps."

An epitaph was placed above his resting place that read: "Pig's Dead, Dog Gone."

Gone maybe, but definitely not forgotten. In 2001, 78 years after his demise, a second memorial service was held for Pig the Dog on campus.

ALMA MATER

The official Alma Mater of the University of Texas is "The Eyes of Texas." It's the third-greatest original manuscript in American history—after the Declaration of Independence and the Constitution, of course—and hangs in the Alumni Center for all good and loyal Texans to salute.

John Sinclair penned it in 1903 after being given a very short time to put it together. He borrowed a well-known saying by university president "Colonel" William Lambdin Prather, who often addressed crowds with the words "The eyes of Texas are

upon you." Sinclair melded his lyrics to the tune "I've Been Working on the Railroad" to create the song we love today, the song played before and after every UT sporting event and other school functions.

The lyrics are:

> *The Eyes of Texas are upon you,*
> *All the live long day.*
> *The Eyes of Texas are upon you,*
> *You can not get away.*
> *Do not think you can escape them*
> *At night or early in the morn—*
> *The Eyes of Texas are upon you*
> *'Til Gabriel blows his horn.*

A very catchy tune with just a hint of Big Brother.

TEXAS FIGHT

"The Eyes of Texas" is often followed by another song called "Texas Fight," otherwise known as "TAPS." It's played after touchdowns and even extra points, and is the official fight song of UT. Colonel Walter S. Hunnicutt wrote it along with James E. King, with lyrics provided by longtime Longhorn Band director Blondie Pharr. The song actually begins as a faster version of the song played at military funerals—perhaps because it heralds Texas scores and the end of all hope for the other team.

The lyrics are:

Texas fight, Texas fight,
And it's good-bye to A&M.
Texas fight, Texas fight,
And we'll put over one more win.
Texas fight, Texas fight,
For it's Texas that we love best.
Hail, hail, the gang's all here,
And it's good-bye to all the rest!
(YELL)
Yea Orange! Yea White!
Yea Longhorns! Fight! Fight! Fight!
Texas fight! Texas fight,
Yea Texas fight!
Texas fight! Texas fight,
Yea Texas fight!

A famous ESPN commercial had analyst Kirk Herbstreit making up new lyrics to the song, which prompted head coach Mack Brown to chastise him, saying, "We don't free-style 'Texas Fight,' big boy." Which isn't entirely true, since sometimes the line "Hail, hail, the gang's all here" is replaced with "Give 'em hell / Give 'em hell / Go, Horns, go!"

HOOK 'EM HORNS

Cheerleader Harley Clark came up with the iconic Hook 'em Horns salute way back in 1955.

The gesticulating genius based it on Bevo's own horns. But Clark actually got the idea of the hand gesture from another student, Henry Pitts. Clark used his UT education to become

a well-respected judge in Texas, where I'm sure he came to see many other hand gestures, mostly aimed at him.

COLORS

The school colors of burnt orange and white came about because of baseball, a quick-thinking entrepreneur, and two boys late for a train.

In April of 1885, on a fine Saturday morning, the baseball squad and their fans boarded a train in Austin bound for Georgetown, 30 miles north, for a game against Southwestern University.

Back then men wore colored ribbons on their lapels to show their support for the team. Enterprising young men would wear long ribbons to share with lovely young women who had none of their own.

Just before the train was to depart, it was noticed that no ribbons had been brought, so students Clarence Miller and Venable Proctor jumped off and ran to the nearest store on Congress Avenue. Breathlessly, they asked for two colors of ribbon from the shopkeeper, who asked them which colors they would like. Knowing the train was starting to move out of the station, the boys said any colors would do.

The thrifty shopkeeper gave them white ribbon, because it was so popular and he had plenty, along with bright orange, for the exact opposite reason—it was not very popular, so he had plenty of it cluttering up his general store.

Sadly, the baseball team lost that day.

Despite that charming story, orange and white didn't become the official colors of the school for many years to come. Different coaches used different colors, including gold and white. When that combination was deemed insufficiently masculine, orange and white returned in 1895.

In 1897 the team's laundresses got tired of trying to get the mud out of the white parts of the uniforms, so they switched to maroon because it was better for hiding dirt. Strangely, the 1899 yearbook actually stated that the school colors were gold and maroon!

Finally a vote was held, and orange and white won the day. For 30 years those colors reigned supreme despite the orange fading during the season and looking more like a dingy yellow by the end of the year. By the 1920s other teams were calling the Longhorns "yellow bellies." That did not go over well in Austin.

In 1928 head coach Clyde Littlefield changed the original plain orange to a dark orange, which later became burnt orange, also known as Texas orange. But the darker dye became too expensive during the Depression years of the 1930s, when bright orange returned. It was none other than head coach Darrell Royal who brought back the burnt orange and white during the 1960s.

THE UT TOWER

The 27-story UT Tower is a beloved symbol for both Longhorns and the city of Austin itself.

It was 1937 when physical plant head Carl J. Eckhardt Jr. first lit the tower with orange lights. Since then different lighting schemes have been used to recognize various achievements.

The No. 1 on all four sides lit by orange lights meant the school had won a national championship. The entire tower glowing orange meant a victory over hated Texas A&M. The top of the tower lit in orange meant victories over other schools or a conference title.

These days an elaborate system of lighting schemes exists for both athletic and academic honors, including no lights at all on a darkened tower to designate a solemn occasion, such as the Texas A&M bonfire tragedy.

THE HEX RALLY

In 1941 the Longhorns were in the midst of a jinx. Seems they hadn't won at Kyle Field in College Station against Texas A&M since 1923.

Not leaving any stone unturned, students visited local fortune teller Madame Agusta Hipple and asked her sage advice for ending this curse. She told them to light red candles before the game. And it worked! Texas won the game over the favored Aggies, and a mighty tradition began.

Ever since then, students by the thousands join the team and the band on the steps of the Main Building on campus before the Thanksgiving week game against A&M to sing "The Eyes of Texas" three times as candles are lit throughout the crowd.

It will be interesting to see if this tradition is continued now that the Aggies have run off to the Southeastern Conference with their tails between their legs and no games with A&M are scheduled for the next few years.

SMOKEY THE CANNON

Smokey the Cannon lives in the south end zone. Its shot thunders through the stadium every time the Longhorns score, as well as at the end of every victory.

The Texas Cowboys take care of Smokey, who—reminiscent of most Sooners—reportedly fires blanks. Even so, it seems to point toward College Station and Norman a heck of a lot of the time.

THE TORCHLIGHT PARADE

Yet another part of the tradition surrounding the Texas vs. Texas A&M game, the torchlight parade, started during World War I as part of the rally before the annual contest.

The school's male students would gather for a parade the night before Thanksgiving with homemade torches, marching from the east side of the Forty Acres. Meanwhile, the female students marched from the west carrying many-colored Chinese lanterns on poles (since it was considered too dangerous for ladies to carry torches). The two genders would meet at the south entrance to the old Main Building, where they were joined by fans and alumni. The parade began on Guadalupe Street and made its way to Gregory Gym.

This tradition continued gloriously until the 1960s, when, like so many traditions around the country, it began to be neglected and was finally cancelled altogether. It wasn't until 1987 that the Spirit and Traditions Board, fresh off its successful Hex Rally from the year before, brought back the torches and parade before the annual tilt against Oklahoma.

The Texas Exes Student Chapter now organizes the event, which begins when the sun goes down near the campus' northwest corner. They're joined in the parade by the school's cheerleaders, the Longhorn Band, and other groups, including students and fans.

As in the days of yore, the parade winds its way down Guadalupe Street and, after a twist and turn or two, finds itself in front of the Main Building and Tower for the start of the "Beat OU" football rally.

YELLS

There are many yells associated with the Longhorns. Some have come and gone while some will always be favorites. Here are a few of the ones that have meant the most to Longhorns fans through the decades.

The "Varsity Yell" came about all the way back in 1892:

> *Hullabaloo! Hooray! Hooray!*
> *Hullabaloo! Hooray! Hooray!*
> *HooRAY! HooRAY!*
> *Varsity! Varsity! U. T. A.!*

In 1896, the "Rattle de Thrat Yell" appeared:

> *Rattle de thrat, de thrat, de thrat!*
> *Rattle de thrat, de thrat, de thrat!*
> *Longhorn! Cactus Thorn!*
> *Moooooooooooo Texas!*

And 1895 saw the invention of the "Texas Football Yell":

> *Rah! Rah! Rah!*
> *Who are we?*
> *Texas! U of T!*
> *Rough, tough,*
> *We're the stuff.*
> *We play football,*
> *Never get enough. Rah!*

Then there's the "Lollapaloose Yell" of 1898 (not to be confused with Lollapalooza):

> *Coyote cayuse!*
> *Lollapaloose!*
> *Everybody yell!*
> *Turn Texas loose!*

The "Nine Rahs Yell" began making the rounds in 1906. It's short and to the point:

> *Rah! Rah! Rah!*
> *Rah! Rah! Rah!*
> *Rah! Rah! Rah!*

And in 1950, the "Whisper Chant" hit Austin:

T – T – T – E – X
X – X – X – A – S
T – E – X
X – A – S
Texas!
Fight!

DARREL K. ROYAL–TEXAS MEMORIAL STADIUM

The Darrell K. Royal–Texas Memorial Stadium is the home of the Texas Longhorns on autumn Saturdays. Originally dedicated on Thanksgiving Day of 1924—and christened with a 7–0 win over Texas A&M in front of 35,000 fans—it was originally named Memorial Stadium in honor of the 5,280 Texans who died serving their country in World War I, as well as the almost 200,000 Texans who served in the conflict. It was rededicated in 1977 to honor veterans who have served in all wars. The name of legendary coach Darrell K. Royal was added in 1996.

The first night game there was played on September 17, 1955. Unfortunately, the 47,000 in attendance saw the Longhorns fall to Texas Tech 20–14.

The stadium itself has been around quite a while, but upgrades and renovations have maintained it as one of the best facilities in all of college football. A state-of-the-art locker room, which even includes a gaming lounge where players can relax, was added in 2011.

Longhorns fans flash the "Hook 'em Horns" sign during pregame festivities prior to the Texas–Texas Tech game in 2011 at Darrell K. Royal–Texas Memorial Stadium. The Horns whupped Tech 52–20. Photo courtesy of Getty Images

An expansion in 2009 brought the stadium's capacity to more than 100,000 fans; in fact, it is now the largest college stadium in the southwest, with only five other college stadiums bigger in the entire nation. The largest crowd on record to gather there was the 101,624 fans who saw the victory over Rice on September 3, 2011.

FieldTurf was installed in the stadium in 2009, giving it the capacity to be used for other purposes besides football. Before that, the team played on natural grass from 1924 to 1968 and

artificial turf from 1969 to 1996, when they returned to natural grass.

The stadium's scoreboard is the largest in college football and one of the largest in the nation—the better to see all those UT touchdowns.

The Longhorns have a .778 winning percentage in DKR-Texas Memorial Stadium, having won 348 games there from 1924 through 2011. Before that the team played at Clark Field on campus from 1896 to 1924, where they won 136 games for a .862 winning percentage. And before even Clark Field, UT was 12–1 at home from 1893 to 1895.

The team's all-time home record stands at 498–120–12, which is a .803 winning percentage as of the end of the 2011 season.

6

WE LOVE LONGHORNS LORE

INSPIRING STORIES

The October 10, 1998, game against OU was special for two reasons.

First, Texas routed Oklahoma 34–3. It was also a special game for running back Ricky Williams and the family of legendary Southern Methodist University running back Doak Walker. It was a game in which a Longhorn honored a fallen Mustang.

Williams had won the Doak Walker Award, which is given to the best running back in the nation, during the previous season. SMU great and 1948 Heisman Trophy winner Walker had become friends with Williams around the same time.

Not too long after they met in January of 1998, Walker had a tragic skiing accident that left him paralyzed and would later lead to the 71-year-old NFL Hall of Famer's death. Two weeks after his friend's passing, Williams took the field against the Sooners wearing No. 37 instead of his usual No. 34 in honor of Walker. The Cotton Bowl is sometimes actually referred to as "the House that Doak Built" because of the legendary games the Mustangs played there.

It was an emotional day for Williams, who had found Walker's humility and love for life inspiring. He rushed for 139 yards and two touchdowns, pointing to his heart and then the sky to honor his friend.

After the game, Coach Mack Brown and the players presented Walker's family with the game ball in a very emotional locker room. Williams gave them his soiled game jersey, apologizing for its blood-stained and dirty appearance.

It was a game and a moment that transcended teams and time.

AMUSING TALES

Bobby Layne is a name emblazoned in the minds of fans of both the Texas Longhorns and the NFL's Detroit Lions. His hard-playing and hard-partying ways made him a legend. Layne was one of the last NFL players to play without a face mask. He's even credited with putting a curse on an entire team—and it worked!

Layne grew up in Dallas, where Doak Walker was one of his childhood friends and teammates. Walker would go on to fame at SMU, while Layne made a name for himself at UT from 1944 through 1947.

Layne made the All-American team and was also a pitcher on the Longhorns baseball team. He never lost a game and even threw two no-hitters. Despite offers from three major league baseball teams—the Cardinals, the Red Sox, and the New York Giants—Layne decided to play for the NFL because he thought he'd make it big more quickly that way.

Drafted by George Halas' legendary Bears, Layne had difficulty getting any playing time behind the likes of Sid Luckman and Johnny Lujack. So he made a move to the Detroit Lions, where his career took off. His old friend Doak Walker would later join him with that team.

Layne had rather firm beliefs as to how football should be played, and one of them was that the quarterback always calls the plays. This led him to argue with head coach Bo McMillin, so much so that the team bought out McMillin's contract and hired Buddy Parker to replace him. Parker saw eye to eye with Layne. The partnership worked out: Layne took the Lions to an NFL championship title in 1952. They won it again the next year, but a three-peat was not in the cards, as they fell in the title game of 1954.

Layne had a reputation for hard partying; in fact, one story has it that two linemen once had to pick him up by the legs and dunk him headfirst into a barrel of water just to wake him up in time to play a game.

In 1957 Detroit was on its way to another title game when bad luck hit Layne. He broke his leg in three places during a game; his backup, Tobin Rote, was the one to lead the Lions to another title. The next year the team wanted Layne to split playing time with Rote, which didn't sit well with Layne. So the team decided to trade him to Pittsburgh, where he finished his career.

Layne thought he had been treated rather shabbily, and therefore reportedly placed a curse on the Lions that they wouldn't win another championship for 50 years. As any Lions fan can

tell you, the curse has worked so far! In fact, it's been longer than 50 years.

In 2009 Detroit drafted quarterback Matthew Stafford out of the University of Georgia. Stafford, like Layne, is from Dallas; he even played football at the same high school as Layne. Maybe this Texas-raised boy can finally break the curse of another Texas boy.

In 1967 Layne was inducted into the Pro Football Hall of Fame, and the next year he went into the College Football Hall of Fame.

NOVEMBER 14, 1936, AT MEMORIAL STADIUM IN MINNEAPOLIS, MINNESOTA

The unranked Longhorns faced a daunting battle against the second-ranked Golden Gophers in this road game. It didn't help matters that head coach Jack Chevigny had announced during the week of the game that he would be stepping down as coach at the end of the season.

And it didn't go well for most of the game, as Texas fell to the eventual national champion Minnesota team 47–19. But kick returner Hugh Wolfe did earn one fleeting moment of glory for the team.

The Longhorn ran a kick back 95 yards for a touchdown—a team record that would stand for 42 seasons. Wolfe's description of the play was downright amusing: "The kickoff return was a fluke. I picked out the biggest one and ran straight at him, faked left, then cut right to see nothing but daylight and

the man who held the ball for the kick. He was just getting to his feet when I said 'good-bye.' Shirley Temple could have made that TD." (For those of you under retirement age, Shirley Temple was a child movie star back in the 1930s and 1940s.)

NOVEMBER 9, 1963, AT MEMORIAL STADIUM IN AUSTIN

The Longhorns came in as the top-ranked team in the country this time around, and lived up to the hype by shutting out Baylor 7–0 on the way to an undefeated season and their first ever national title. Baylor came into the game tied with Texas in the Southwest Conference at 4–0. The Bears led the conference in offense, but couldn't score that day against the stout UT defense.

Safety Duke Carlisle (who also played quarterback that season) made the play that saved the championship season by closing ground on a wide-open Bears receiver by the name of Lawrence Elkins, who was running a post pattern. Carlisle jumped in front of Elkins in the end zone and intercepted the pass with just 29 seconds left in the game. The play was a miracle in more than one way. When studying film of the play afterward, the coaches noticed it had a remarkable effect on two fans. A boy standing on crutches behind the end zone raised both crutches in the air, and a woman sitting in a wheelchair threw aside her blanket and leapt to her feet in celebration. Chalk it up to the healing power of Texas football.

7
WE LOVE AUSTIN
AND ALL OF TEXAS

THE LONGHORNS CERTAINLY have their share of famous alumni.

The University of Spoiled Children (USC) has more star fans, but that's only because their armed compound is within easy driving distance of Hollywood.

Three Texas fans that come to mind include one of the world's most famous actors, one of the world's greatest athletes, and a person who was the most powerful man in the world not too long ago.

I'm talking about Matthew McConaughey, Lance Armstrong, and former President George W. Bush.

MATTHEW McCONAUGHEY

Here's a guy who loves UT so much that he still has a home in Austin despite being able to afford to park his Airstream RV anywhere he wants to. And he still lives there despite being arrested by the Austin police for the little indiscretion of

playing his bongos too loud—while buck naked. (No word on if he was using his drumstick.)

The official charge was resisting arrest, but that just shows the determination embodied by a Longhorn. Just like the Texas players, McConaughey was 100 percent committed to playing those drums that night to the loudest of his ability no matter what the price.

Sports Illustrated named him as No. 2 on their list of famous college football fans and described him thus:

> Matthew McConaughey, Texas. Romantic comedies and Longhorns football games are the most likely places to spot this native Texan. McConaughey also likes to stop by practice to chat with Mack Brown or break the team huddle. On game days in Austin, he and buddy Lance Armstrong often watch from the sideline like a couple of 40-year-old frat boys.

Football is in McConaughey's blood. (Unfortunately for him, it is not in his arms or legs.) He was born in Texas, the son of a former Green Bay Packer draft pick. He was also *People* magazine's "Sexiest Man Alive" for 2005. And did you see the movie *Reign of Fire*? Did you see those abs?! Makes you want to hit the floor and do some sit ups. He's in better shape than half the OU football team. McConaughey is also the commercial spokesman for beefcake—oops, I mean beef.

McConaughey played an inspirational coach in one of the best films ever made about football and what it can mean to a community, *We Are Marshall*. I dare you to watch that

entire movie and not get a lump in your throat more than once, especially during the first 15 minutes. McConaughey portrays Coach Jack Lengyel, who rebuilt the Thundering Herd team after a plane crash killed most of the players and coaching staff in 1970.

McConaughey matriculated at the University of Texas at Austin from 1989 to 1993. For you Oklahoma fans, that means he attended classes there and, unlike you, graduated.

He started school there after spending some time in Australia, so when he first hit the Austin campus, he was sporting a fake Aussie accent authentic enough to fool all his friends and teachers—that is until his parents outed him as a boy from the south of Texas during Parents Day.

After Hurricane Katrina devastated Louisiana and Mississippi, McConaughey rescued hundreds of dogs, cats, and even hamsters. (You'd be amazed how many of them you can fit in a sack—hamsters, I mean.) He was once driving through the rough streets of Sherman Oaks, California, when he saw two boys putting hairspray on a cat and trying to set if aflame. He jumped out of his car and wrestled that puss away, then gave the boys a stern lecture. Everyone knows cats prefer to do their own hair.

Not too long ago McConaughey auctioned off his motorcycle for charity. But this wasn't just any motorcycle, mind you—it was a 2007 commemorative Texas Longhorn–themed Bobber Motorcycle, made by the Knockout Motorcycle Company in honor of UT's national title.

McConaughey loves prowling the sideline at Texas games. In fact, Coach Brown has said that if he let him, McConaughey would call every play from the sideline. He's also been seen giving the Hook 'em Horns sign during several Texas bowl games, including the national championship game win over the Trojans on January 4, 2006, in Rose Bowl stadium. At least I think that was a Hook 'em Horns sign. Maybe he was saluting their No. 1 status. Or maybe he spotted Coach Barry Switzer in the stands.

If you're lucky, you may spot McConaughey jogging around Malibu sporting the Texas colors. (If you don't see him, you're still lucky—you're hanging out in Malibu!)

Matthew McConaughey auctioned off his commemorative 2007 Texas Longhorn–themed Bobber Motorcycle for charity. It was made in honor of Texas' national championship. Photo courtesy of the Knockout Motorcycle Company

Yes, McConaughey is Texan through and through, as this quote from imdb.com shows:

> To understand me, you need to understand Texan logic. If you come from Texas, you're 100 percent American, but you'll do things the Texan way. We're independent. We've got our own way of doing things. Try to build fences round us and we'll run you out of town. I can go anywhere in the world but my spirit is still Texan and I recognize my own kind. There are no secret handshakes, but when Texans meet, there's a special fraternity.

McConaughey once told Oprah Winfrey that watching Texas beat Southern Cal in the Rose Bowl for the national championship made him feel better than he imagined winning an Oscar would!

LANCE ARMSTRONG

As seven-time winner of the greatest bicycle race in the world, the Tour de France, Lance Armstrong is one of the most famous athletes in history.

But more importantly, he hails from Texas, lives in Austin, and is a lifelong Longhorns fan. He's also an inspiration for cancer survivors everywhere, having beaten the deadly disease before winning all those races, and his tireless efforts as chairman of the Lance Armstrong Foundation (famous for their yellow "Livestrong" bracelets) have raised both money and awareness in the battle against cancer.

From 1999 through 2005, Armstrong won the Tour de France an amazing seven times in a row. No other man has won more than five times in a row. He also won ESPN's ESPY Award as Best Male Athlete from 2003 to 2006.

Armstrong loves attending UT games and can often be seen roaming the sideline (on foot, not on a bike). One must wonder if he ever gets the urge to jump up on one of the training cycles. He even appeared on ESPN's *College GameDay* program in 2006, when the show broadcast from Austin.

PRESIDENT GEORGE W. BUSH

The final celebrity in our triumvirate of famous Longhorn fans is none other than the former leader of the free world, the 43rd president of the United States, George W. Bush. Bush was president from 2001 to 2009. His father, George H.W. Bush, was the 41st president.

Bush was born in Connecticut while his father was attending college at Yale, but the family soon moved to Midland, Texas, where George W. could root for a winning football program. One of his daughters eventually graduated from UT, and the two of them were photographed making the Hook 'em Horns sign during his second inaugural parade in 2005 in Washington, D.C.

He welcomed the 2005 National Champion Longhorns to the White House on Valentine's Day in 2006.

The team gave the president a bronze football to commemorate the title, and Mr. Bush told Coach Brown that he was

President George W. Bush gives the "Hook 'em Horns" sign while holding his Longhorns jersey with coach Mack Brown at a White House ceremony to honor the 2005 national champions on February 14, 2006.

following in the footsteps of legendary football coach Darrell Royal at Texas. (Brown, not the president.)

He even joked with trainer Jeff "Mad Dog" Madden that he didn't know Madden owned a suit. Mr. Bush then joked with Vince Young, whose suit didn't arrive in time for the ceremony.

Mr. Bush also praised fullback Ahmard Hall, a Marine who served in Afghanistan and Kosovo before returning to play football at UT.

JOKES WE LOVE

Little Bobby was in his fourth-grade classroom when the teacher asked the children what their fathers did for a living. All the typical answers came up: policeman, fireman, etc. Bobby was being unusually quiet, so the teacher asked him about his father. "My father is an exotic dancer in a gay club and takes off all his clothes in front of other men. If the money is really good, he'll go out to the alley with some guy and make love with him for money." The shaken teacher hurriedly put the other children to work on some coloring and took Bobby aside to ask him, "Is that really true about your father?" "No," said Bobby. "He coaches at the University of Oklahoma. But I was too embarrassed to say that in front of the other kids."

Why can't Bob Stoops eat ice cream? Because he chokes when gets near a bowl.

How do you find a stupid person in a crowd? Yell out, "Boomer!"

What do you call the sweat on two Sooners having sex? Relative humidity.

Oklahoma coach Bob Stoops has decided to dress only 20 players for their next game. The other players will have to dress themselves.

Why is it so difficult to solve a murder in Norman, Oklahoma? There are no dental records and all the DNA is the same.

How many OU freshmen does it take to screw in a light bulb? None. That's a sophomore course.

What do you call a crime ring in Norman? A huddle.

Sooners head coach Bob Stoops was visiting a class in an elementary school. They were discussing words and their meanings. The teacher asked the coach if he would like to lead the discussion on the word *tragedy*. So Stoops asked the class for an example of one. One little boy stood up and said, "If my best friend, who lives on a farm, is playing in the field and a tractor runs over him and kills him, that would be a tragedy." "No," said Stoops, "that would be an accident." A little girl raised her hand. "If a school bus carrying 50 children drove over a cliff and killed everyone inside, that would be a tragedy." "I'm afraid not," explained Stoops. "That's what we would call a great loss." The room went silent. No other children volunteered. Stoops searched the room. "Isn't there someone here who can give me an example of a tragedy?" Finally, at the back of the room, Little Stewie raised his hand. In a quiet voice he said, "If the plane carrying you and the Sooners football team was struck by a friendly fire missile and blown to smithereens, that would be a tragedy." "Fantastic!" exclaimed Stoops. "That's right. And can you tell me why that would be a tragedy?" "Well," said the boy, "it has to be a tragedy, because it certainly wouldn't be a great loss, and it probably wouldn't be a freaking accident, either."

Three Sooners were driving in a car: a quarterback, a punter, and a linebacker. Who was driving? The police.

Two OU football players were hootin' and hollerin' when their friend asked them why they were celebrating. The smart one said proudly that they had just finished a jigsaw puzzle and it only took two months. "Two months!?"

exclaimed the friend. "To complete a simple puzzle?" The Sooner replied, "Yeah, but the box said '4–6 years.'"

Did you hear about the Oklahoma player who got kicked off the team? He was caught with a book.

Two Sooners were walking in downtown Norman when they came across a dog licking himself, as dogs are wont to do. One Sooner looked down and said, "Boy, I sure wish I could do that." The second Sooner said, "You better pet him first."

A general was walking through the desert when he came across an old lamp. Upon rubbing the lamp, a genie popped out and told the general that he would grant him a wish for freeing him. The general pulled out a map and said, "Show me on this map where the enemy is and help us win the war." The genie replied, "I'm sorry, but I'm not that powerful of a genie. Do you have another wish?" The general thought for a minute, then said, "Well, can you make Oklahoma win a bowl game?" The genie pondered that for a moment, then said, "Let me see that map again."

An OU graduate was driving home from work when his cell phone rang. He answered it and his wife was on the line. "Honey," she said, "I just wanted to warn you, I'm watching the news and there's some idiot driving on the wrong side of the road on the highway." The OU grad replied, "You're wrong, it's not one idiot—it's hundreds of them!"

What's the only sign of intelligent life in Norman? "Austin: 187 miles."

Albert Einstein went to a party and introduced himself to a woman, saying, "Hi, I'm Albert Einstein. What's your IQ?" "Two hundred and forty," she replied. "Great, we can discuss the mysteries of the universe. We have a lot we can talk about," he replied. Later he walked up to a man and said, "Hi, I'm Albert Einstein. What's your IQ?" "One hundred and forty-five," the man replied. "Great, we can talk about thermodynamics," said Einsten. Later he was talking to another gentleman and said, "Hi, I'm Albert Einstein. What's your IQ? "Forty-three," the man replied. Einstein got a puzzled look on his face for a minute, then exclaimed, "Boomer Sooner!"

What does the average OU student get on his SAT test? Drool.

What does a Longhorn call duct tape? Sooner chrome.

TEXAS TWEETS AND OTHER SOCIAL MEDIA

Longhorn fans pride themselves on using the latest technology and social media to learn and talk about their beloved team. From Twitter to Facebook to blogging, the Internet is awash with information about UT. Here are some of the more interesting sites to check out.

TWITTER FEEDS

- ★ MBTexasFootball, the official Twitter page of Texas Football and MackBrown-TexasFootball.com
- ★ alcalde.texasexes.org
- ★ texasbuzztap
- ★ ESPNHornsNation

* Suzhalliburton
* JNewbergESPN
* JeffHowe247
* Bevobeat
* GhostofBigRoy

FACEBOOK PAGES

* Texas Longhorns
* Texas Longhorns Football

BLOGS

* Burntorangenation.com
* Blog.chron.com, from the *Houston Chronicle*
* Statesman.com, the *Austin American-Statesman* newspaper
* The college newspaper can be seen at dailytexan. online.com
* fanblogs.com/big12/texas/
* hookemreport.com
* sbnation.com/ncaa-football/teams/texas-longhorns
* sportsnipe.com/texas_football
* dallasnews.com/sports/college-sports/, the *Dallas Morning News* newspaper

LONGHORNS ADORE AUSTIN

Austin, Texas, not only has the extreme good luck to be the home city of the beautiful University of Texas at Austin campus, it's also the capital city of the great state of Texas.

The self-proclaimed "Live Music Capital of the World," Austin is home to both the famous South by Southwest music festival

and the PBS television concert series *Austin City Limits*. It's also the seat of Travis County, located in central Texas. It's the fourth-largest city in the state and the 14th-largest in the nation, with just under 800,000 residents.

Austinites have a motto for their town: "Keep Austin Weird." They pride themselves on having a live-and-let-live attitude. The Marlboro Man, however, is not particularly welcome, since much of the city is now a nonsmoking area.

Located on the banks of the Colorado River, the area that would eventually become Austin had been inhabited for more than 10,000 years prior to the arrival of white settlers. Members of the Comanche tribe were dominant. The actual city was founded by settlers during the 1830s and was first named Waterloo. It was designated as the capital of the Republic of Texas in 1839, and was then renamed in honor of the father of Texas, Stephen F. Austin. A rivalry with Houston was born over arguments as to where the capital should be located, which explains the animosity that survives to this day between UT and the universities of Rice and Houston.

Austin is now the home of many Fortune 500 companies, including Whole Foods, and is a hub for technology-based businesses. It's the largest city in America without a major professional sports team—but that's okay, since the Longhorns provide so much sports entertainment. It's also got a minor league hockey team called the Ice Bats, whose name was inspired by the city's distinction of having the largest urban bat colony in North America. These bats call the Congress Avenue Bridge over Town Lake in downtown Austin their home; during certain evenings, more than a million Mexican

free-tail bats swarm out from underneath the bridge to the delight of locals and tourists alike. That's a lot of bat guano.

UNIVERSITY of TEXAS at AUSTIN CAMPUS

September 15, 1883, is a great day in the history of the University of Texas at Austin. That's when the university first opened, although classes did not begin until the next year. The school now boasts nearly half a million alumni and hands out 12,000 degrees annually.

More than 50,000 students enjoy the seventeen libraries and seven museums that the campus boasts. The university employs around 24,000 people including faculty, with an operating budget of over $2 billion a year. That's more than the gross national product of nations such as Mongolia, Monaco, the British Virgin Islands, and Micronesia. In fact, that's more money than the GNP of the countries of Liberia, Gambia, and Equatorial Guinea *combined*.

NATIONAL CHAMPION LONGHORNS

1963: Texas began the season ranked fifth in the Associated Press poll, but like a rocket ship countdown, they climbed a rung on the ladder every week. By the fifth week of the season, they were at No. 1 to stay. What made it even sweeter was the 28–7 upset win over then-top-ranked Oklahoma that propelled the Longhorns to the top spot. UT, already named the national champions by the AP, completed their first national title season with 11 wins and no losses by defeating second-ranked Navy in the Cotton Bowl, 28–6.

LONGHORN LOUNGES
(*IN NO PARTICULAR ORDER*)

Vince Young Steakhouse, 301 San Jacinto Boulevard, Austin
Champions Restaurant and Sports Bar, 300 E. 4th Street, Austin
Third Base Sports Bar, West Sixth Street, Austin
Cover 3, 2700 W. Anderson Lane, Ste 202, Austin
Scholz Garten, 1607 San Jacinto Boulevard, Austin
Doc's MotorWorks Bar & Grill, 1123 S. Congress Ave
   (South Congress & Academy), Austin

T E X A S

1969: What better way to celebrate 100 years of Texas football than with their second national title. Beginning the season ranked fourth, UT didn't reach the top of the polls until mid-November after a 69–7 trouncing of SMU. In the last game of the regular season, known as "The Game of the Century," the Longhorns nipped second-ranked Arkansas 15–14 in Fayetteville. The team rallied around safety Fred Steinmark, who underwent surgery a week after the game to amputate a leg because of bone cancer. President Richard M. Nixon attended the game and presented the Texas coaches and players with a plaque afterward naming them the national champions. They ended a perfect 11–0 season by beating ninth-ranked Notre Dame in the Cotton Bowl, 21–17. It was the first time the Fighting Irish had agreed to play in a postseason bowl in 44 seasons. Guess they should have waited another year.

1970: Despite winning the national title the year before, Texas began this season ranked second behind Ohio State. On October 3, their 22-game winning streak was in deep

UNDEFEATED SEASONS

2005:	13–0 under Coach Mack Brown
1969:	11–0 under Coach Darrell Royal
1963:	11–0 under Coach Darrell Royal
1923:	8–0–1 under Coach E.J. Stewart
1920:	9–0–0 under Coach Berry Whitaker
1918:	9–0–0 under Coach Bill Juneau
1914:	8–0–0 under Coach Dave Allerdice
1900:	6–0–0 under Coach S.H. Thompson
1895:	5–0–0 under Coach Frank Crawford
1893:	4–0–0 with no head coach

jeopardy. No. 13 UCLA had held Texas' wishbone offense, and the Bruins led 17–13 with only 25 seconds left to play. But Cotton Speyrer saved the day by catching a long touchdown pass from Longhorns quarterback Eddie Phillips for a 20–17 victory. A 45–21 spanking of Rice on October 24 then sent UT to No. 1. The regular season ended with an easy 42–7 win over the fourth-ranked Razorbacks, and it was on to a rematch with No. 6 Notre Dame in the Cotton Bowl. The Fighting Irish upset Texas 24–11, ending their 30-game winning streak. The loss dropped UT to third in the AP poll, but United Press International (UPI) named them the national champions.

2005: Thirty-five years is a long time to wait between national titles, but that's how long it took to bring UT back to that spotlight. After losing the Heisman Trophy to Southern Cal's Reggie Bush, Texas quarterback Vince Young got sweet revenge by defeating Bush's top-ranked USC team for the national

championship and the Bowl Championship Series title in what many call the greatest college football game ever played. Young scored three touchdowns while passing for 267 yards and rushing for 200 more to lead second-ranked UT to a 41–38 upset over the Trojans in the Rose Bowl. The win snapped a 34-game winning streak for Southern Cal and capped a 13–0 perfect season for the Longhorns.

FAMOUS ALUMNI AND STUDENTS OF THE UNIVERSITY OF TEXAS

F. Murray Abraham: Born in 1939 in Pittsburgh, Pennsylvania, Abraham is an actor best known for his role in the movie *Amadeus*, for which he won an Oscar. His other film roles include *Last Action Hero, Scarface, Thirteen Ghosts, Star Trek: Insurrection,* and *The Name of the Rose.* He attended UT at El Paso and Austin.

James Baker: Born in 1930 in Houston, Texas, Baker is the former secretary of state under President George H.W. Bush from 1989 to 1992. He managed Ronald Reagan's successful campaign for president in 1980 and served as secretary of the treasury under Reagan during the 1980s. He was also the White House chief of staff for both President Ronald Reagan and President George H.W. Bush. He served in the United States Marine Corps from 1952 to 1954 and earned a J.D. degree from UT Law School in 1957.

Alan Bean: Born in 1932 in Wheeler, Texas, Bean is an astronaut and an artist, and is known for being the fourth man to walk on the moon. Bean earned a B.S. degree in aeronautical engineering at UT in 1955.

INTERNATIONAL JOINTS WITH "LONGHORN" IN THEIR NAME

Longhorns Sports Bar, Karachi, Pakistan
Texas Longhorn, Fleminggatan 27, Stockholm 11226, Sweden
Texas Longhorn Grill and Bar, 803 Dundas St. E, Mississauga, Ontario, L4Y2B7, Canada

William J. Bennett: Born in 1943 in Brooklyn, New York, Bennett is a radio talk show host and author. He served as secretary of education under President Ronald Reagan and drug czar under President George H.W. Bush. Bean earned a Ph.D. in philosophy at UT.

Jeb Bush: Born in 1953 in Midland, Texas, Jeb Bush is the former governor of the state of Florida. He is also the son of former President George H.W. Bush and the younger brother of former President George W. Bush. Bush earned a degree in Latin American affairs at UT.

Laura Bush: Born in 1946 in Midland, Texas, Laura Bush was the first lady of the United States from 2001 to 2009. She is married to former President George W. Bush, who is also a former governor of Texas. She is a librarian who earned a master's degree in library science at UT.

Roy Crane: Born in Abilene, Texas, in 1901, Crane was the creator of the comic strip "Buz Sawyer" and one of the defining

artists of American newspaper comics. Crane attended UT before traveling the world as a sailor and later a hobo. He also created the Roy Crane Award in the Arts at the University of Texas in 1965. He died in 1977.

Walter Cronkite: Born in St. Joseph, Missouri, in 1916, Cronkite was a journalist, broadcaster, and author, as well as the anchorman of the CBS *Evening News* from 1962 until his retirement in 1981. He was famous for his nightly signoff of "And that's the way it is." Cronkite covered World War II and the Nuremberg Trials in Europe for the United Press. He left his studies at UT in 1935 to work for the *Houston Post* newspaper. Cronkite died in 2009.

Farrah Fawcett: Born in Corpus Christi, Texas, in 1947, Fawcett was an actress best known for her roles in the television series *Charlie's Angels* and the TV film *The Burning Bed*. She also appeared in the feature film *The Apostle*. Fawcett was formerly married to actors Lee Majors and Ryan O'Neal. She graduated with a degree in microbiology from UT. Fawcett died in 2009.

Peri Gilpin: Born in 1961 in Waco, Texas, Gilpin is an actress best known for her role in the television series *Frasier* from 1993 to 2004. She studied drama at UT.

Jon Hamm: Born in 1971 in St. Louis, Missouri, Hamm is an actor most famous for his role as advertising executive Don Draper in the television show *Mad Men*. Hamm turned down offers to play football in the Ivy League. He studied at UT, but left after his father died during his sophomore year.

Marcia Gay Harden: Born in 1959 in La Jolla, California, Hayden is an actress who has appeared in movies including *Miller's Crossing* and *Pollock*. Her father was in the navy, so she traveled the world before earning a degree in drama at UT.

Lady Bird Johnson: Born in 1912 in Karnack, Texas, Johnson was the first lady of the United States from 1963 to 1969 as the wife of former President Lyndon B. Johnson. Her real name was Claudia Alta, but her nursemaid once said she was "as purty as a lady bird" at an early age, and the name stuck. An early environmentalist, Johnson was responsible for the Highway Beautification Act of 1965. She earned a BA at UT in 1933 with a major in history, then went on to earn a journalism degree in 1934.

Janis Joplin: Born in 1943 in Port Arthur, Texas, Joplin was a singer and a member of the rock bands Big Brother and the Holding Company and Kosmic Blues Band. She performed at the Woodstock music festival in 1969. Her best known songs include "Me and Bobby McGee," "Piece of My Heart," and "Mercedes Benz." She was inducted into the Rock and Roll Hall of Fame in 1995. Joplin was the high school classmate of former Dallas Cowboys coach Jimmy Johnson. She attended UT during the early 1960s, and was known for playing the autoharp in Austin bars. She died in 1970.

Jayne Mansfield: Born in Bryn Mawr, Pennsylvania, in 1933, Mansfield was an actress known for such movies as *Will Success Spoil Rock Hunter?*, *Illegal*, *The Girl Can't Help It*, *The Sheriff of Fractured Jaw*, and *Pete Kelly's Blues*. She took drama classes at UT during the early 1950s. Mansfield died in 1967.

Fess Parker: Born in Fort Worth, Texas, in 1924, Parker is an actor, producer, director, and winery owner who was best known for his roles as Davy Crockett and Daniel Boone in television and movies. Parker earned a degree in history from UT in 1950. Parker died in 2010.

Dennis Quaid: Born in 1954 in Houston, Texas, Quaid is a prolific actor who has appeared in many movies, including *Breaking Away, The Right Stuff, Jaws 3-D, Any Given Sunday, The Long Riders, The Big Easy, D.O.A., Great Balls of Fire!*, and *Wyatt Earp*. Quaid was formerly married to actress Meg Ryan and is the younger brother of actor Randy Quaid. He dropped out of UT in 1974 to move to Los Angeles and pursue an acting career.

Sam Rayburn: Born in Roane County, Tennessee, in 1882, Rayburn's family moved to Texas in 1887. He served as a member of the U.S. House of Representatives from 1913 to 1961 and was speaker of the house three different times, holding that office for 17 years altogether. Rayburn cowrote the bill enacting Rural Electrification and served as a mentor to former President Lyndon B. Johnson. He attended UT Law School during the early 1900s and was admitted to the state bar of Texas in 1908. Rayburn died in 1961.

Mary Lou Retton: Born in 1968 in Fairmont, West Virginia, Retton is a gymnast best known for winning the gold medal for the all-around event during the 1984 Olympic Games in L.A., becoming the first American woman to do so. She won five medals at those games, more than any other athlete attending. Famous for her pixie haircut, she was nicknamed "America's Sweetheart." Retton attended UT after the 1984 Olympics.

Tex Ritter: Born in Murvaul, Texas, in 1905, Ritter was an actor and singer and father of the late actor John Ritter. Known as "America's Most Beloved Cowboy," Ritter was a singing cowboy in B movies during the 1930s and 1940s. He married his leading lady, Dorothy Fay. He later became a country music star in Nashville, and was eventually inducted into the Country Music Hall of Fame in 1964. Ritter also sang the theme song from the film *High Noon*. Ritter studied law at UT. He died in 1974.

Robert Rodriguez: Born in 1968 in San Antonio, Texas, Rodriguez is the director of films such as *From Dusk to Dawn*, *Desperado*, *Sin City*, and *Spy Kids*. He studied film at UT.

Tex Schramm: Born in San Gabriel, California, in 1920, Schramm was the president and general manager of the Dallas Cowboys from 1960 to 1989, during which period he presided over 20 straight winning seasons. He helped the NFL and AFL merge in 1966 and became the assistant director of sports programming for CBS during the late 1950s. Schramm was inducted into the Pro Football Hall of Fame in 1991. He earned a degree in journalism at UT. Schramm died in 2003.

Tommy Tune: Born in 1939 in Wichita Falls, Texas, Tune is an actor, dancer, director, and choreographer, and winner of nine Tony Awards. His best-known shows were *Best Little Whorehouse in Texas* and *The Will Rogers Follies*. Tune majored in drama at UT.

Eli Wallach: Born in 1915 in Brooklyn, New York, Wallach is an actor whose best-known movie roles include *Baby Doll*; *The Magnificent Seven*; *The Misfits*; *How the West Was Won*;

The Good, the Bad, and the Ugly; *Mackenna's Gold*; *The Deep*; *Tough Guys*; and *The Two Jakes*. He was one of three actors to portray Mr. Freeze on the 1960s TV show *Batman*. Wallach served as a captain in the Army Medical Administrative Corps during World War II. He graduated with a B.A. from UT in 1936, which he attended before there was an official theater department. Despite this, he costarred in one play during his school years alongside Walter Cronkite.

Owen Wilson: Born in 1968 in Dallas, Texas, Wilson is an actor and screenwriter. He is best known for his roles in the movies *Anaconda*, *Shanghai Noon*, *Meet the Parents*, *Meet the Fockers*, *Night at the Museum*, *Hall Pass*, *Behind Enemy Lines*, *The Royal Tenenbaums*, *Wedding Crashers*, *Zoolander*, and *Starsky & Hutch*. He is also the brother of actor Luke Wilson. Wilson met his friend, director and screenwriter Wes Anderson, at UT, from which he graduated in 1991.

Renee Zellweger: Born in 1969 in Katy, Texas, Zellweger is an actress in movies including *Jerry Maguire*, *Cold Mountain*, *Chicago*, *Bridget Jones' Diary*, *Down With Love*, and *Cinderella Man*. Zellweger was formerly married to country music star Kenny Chesney. She began a degree in journalism at UT before switching to English, and made the dean's list several times.

LONGHORNS IN THE TEXAS HIGH SCHOOL FOOTBALL HALL OF FAME

Anyone who's ever seen the movie or TV show *Friday Night Lights*, or read the best-selling book, knows how important high school football is in the state of Texas. So it's a huge

honor to make the Texas High School Football Hall of Fame. Here is the list of Longhorns who made the grade, as well as when they were inducted and what position they excelled in.

- ★ Joey Aboussie, 1995, running back
- ★ Marty Akins, 1987, quarterback
- ★ Rooster Andrews, 1992, kicker
- ★ Scott Appleton, 1972, tackle
- ★ Bill Atessis, 1995, defensive end
- ★ Leo Baldwin, 1968, defensive tackle
- ★ Bill Bradley, 1985, back
- ★ Charles Brewer, 1998, quarterback
- ★ Earl Campbell, 1983, running back
- ★ Blair Cherry, 1987, coach
- ★ Randall Clay, 1990, back
- ★ Joe Clements, 2010, quarterback
- ★ Jack Collins, 1992, back
- ★ Quan Cosby, 2011, wide receiver
- ★ Jack Crain, 1984, back
- ★ Pat Culpepper, 2011, linebacker
- ★ Chad Daniel, 1969, guard
- ★ Bobby Dillon, 2001, defensive back
- ★ Todd Dodge, 2005, quarterback
- ★ Noble Doss, 1995, back
- ★ Doug English, 1997, defensive tackle
- ★ Walter Fondren, 1984, back
- ★ Tommy Ford, 2005, running back
- ★ Peter Gardere, 2010, quarterback
- ★ Willie Mack Garza, 2001, defensive back
- ★ Chris Gilbert, 1990, running back
- ★ Jerry Gray, 1995, defensive back

- ★ Charlie Haas, 1972, back
- ★ Britt Hager, 2003, linebacker
- ★ Dick Harris, 1985, lineman
- ★ Bohn Hilliard, 1971, back
- ★ Priest Holmes, 2006, running back
- ★ Johnny "Lam" Jones, 2008, wide receiver
- ★ Ernie Koy Jr., 1989, back
- ★ Ted Koy, 2007, back
- ★ Bobby Lackey, 2011, back
- ★ Tom Landry, 1988, defensive back
- ★ Bobby Layne, 1973, quarterback
- ★ Roosevelt Leaks, 2002, running back
- ★ James Lott, 1994, defensive back
- ★ Stan Mauldin, 1970, linebacker
- ★ Steve McMichael, 1992, defensive tackle
- ★ David McWilliams, 1998, coach
- ★ Tommy Nobis, 1984, linebacker
- ★ Alfred Rose, 1998, defensive end
- ★ Wallace Scott, 1998, defensive end
- ★ Brad Shearer, 2007, defensive tackle
- ★ Jerry Sisemore, 1994, offensive tackle
- ★ Bret Stafford, 1979, quarterback
- ★ Harrison Stafford, 1987, lineman
- ★ James Street, 1999, quarterback
- ★ Lance Taylor, 1996, linebacker
- ★ Byron Townsend, 1991, back
- ★ Johnny Treadwell, 2008, guard
- ★ Steve Worster, 1986, back

LONGHORNS IN THE PRO FOOTBALL HALL OF FAME IN CANTON

Earl Campbell, running back, 1978 to 1984 with the Houston Oilers and 1984 to 1985 with the New Orleans Saints. Class of 1991.

Tom Landry, head coach, 1960 to 1988 with the Dallas Cowboys. Class of 1990.

Bobby Layne, quarterback, 1948 with the Chicago Bears, 1949 with the New York Bulldogs, 1950 to 1958 with the Detroit Lions, and 1958 to 1962 with the Pittsburgh Steelers. Class of 1967.

Tex Schramm, administrator, 1947 to 1956 with the Los Angeles Rams, and 1960 to 1989 with the Dallas Cowboys. Class of 1991.

OKLAHOMANS PLAYING FOR THE RIGHT TEAM

Most Longhorns come from Texas. The state has so much talent that there isn't much need to go outside the borders to raid from other states. In fact, of the 115 players on the 2011 roster, 106 hailed from the Lone Star State. Two came from California, one from Louisiana, one from Colorado, one from Ohio, and one from Mexico. Of the 2012 recruiting class of 28, 24 are from Texas, two are from Mississippi, and one each are from Arizona and Louisiana. None are from Oklahoma.

But sometimes a player comes to UT from Oklahoma—a player smart enough to get the heck out of there and receive

a real higher education. Here is the list of these brilliant Oklahomans.

* ★ Demarco Cobbs from Tulsa, junior linebacker.
* ★ Josh Turner from Oklahoma City, sophomore defensive back.
* ★ Matthew Zapata from Stillwater, sophomore safety.

SOURCES

790thezone.com
ajc.com
Alcalde magazine
Austin.citysearch.com
Bam's blog
Barnhart & Durham radio show
Bing.com
Blog.chron.com
Burntorangenation.com
CBSSports.com
Collegefootball.org
Collegefootballpete. blogspot.com
DailyTexanonline.com
Dawgman.com
Espn.go.com
Facebook.com
FoxSports.com
Here Come the Texas Longhorns by Lou Maysel
Hookemreport.com
Imdb.com
Jrsbarbq.com
Jsc.NASA.gov
Lancearmstrong.com

Lostlettermen.com
MackBrown-TexasFootball.com
Newsok.com
Orangebloods.com
OU.edu
Ranker.com
SoonerSports.com
Statesman.com
Survivorposters.com
Texas.rivals.com
Texassports.com
TheDanPatrickShow.com
Barnhart & Durham Show
TonyBarnhart.com
Twitter.com
Wikipedia.com
YouTube.com

ACKNOWLEDGMENTS

I'D LIKE TO THANK Tom Bast and Michael Emmerich of Triumph Books for sending me this assignment. I'd also like to thank Adam Motin for steering this along the right path, and a big round of applause to Alex Lubertozzi of Prologue Publishing Services for doing the heavy lifting of editing this collection of words into the fine product in front of you.

I also want to thank my dogs—Red, Strider, and Bear—for their constant diversions and for keeping my feet warm underneath the desk. Red and Strider passed on just as this book was being finished, and I miss their "Hey, stop typing and come play" looks.

I would like to send a thank you to legendary Texas linebacker Tommy Nobis for giving me and Dad the few reasons we had to cheer during the early days of the Atlanta Falcons. And to Archie Manning, for showing me that your childhood heroes can have just as much class off the field as you thought they did on it.

And to my grandparents, who didn't call the folks with the big net to come get their grandson when he was outside in the yard by himself pretending to be an option quarterback in that most beautiful of college offenses, the wishbone, which both the Longhorns and the Sooners played to perfection.

And in 1950, the "Whisper Chant" hit Austin:

T – T – T – E – X
X – X – X – A – S
T – E – X
X – A – S
Texas!
Fight!

DARREL K. ROYAL–TEXAS MEMORIAL STADIUM

The Darrell K. Royal–Texas Memorial Stadium is the home of the Texas Longhorns on autumn Saturdays. Originally dedicated on Thanksgiving Day of 1924—and christened with a 7–0 win over Texas A&M in front of 35,000 fans—it was originally named Memorial Stadium in honor of the 5,280 Texans who died serving their country in World War I, as well as the almost 200,000 Texans who served in the conflict. It was rededicated in 1977 to honor veterans who have served in all wars. The name of legendary coach Darrell K. Royal was added in 1996.

The first night game there was played on September 17, 1955. Unfortunately, the 47,000 in attendance saw the Longhorns fall to Texas Tech 20–14.

The stadium itself has been around quite a while, but upgrades and renovations have maintained it as one of the best facilities in all of college football. A state-of-the-art locker room, which even includes a gaming lounge where players can relax, was added in 2011.

- ★ Suzhalliburton
- ★ JNewbergESPN
- ★ JeffHowe247
- ★ Bevobeat
- ★ GhostofBigRoy

FACEBOOK PAGES

- ★ Texas Longhorns
- ★ Texas Longhorns Football

BLOGS

- ★ Burntorangenation.com
- ★ Blog.chron.com, from the *Houston Chronicle*
- ★ Statesman.com, the *Austin American-Statesman* newspaper
- ★ The college newspaper can be seen at dailytexan. online.com
- ★ fanblogs.com/big12/texas/
- ★ hookemreport.com
- ★ sbnation.com/ncaa-football/teams/texas-longhorns
- ★ sportsnipe.com/texas_football
- ★ dallasnews.com/sports/college-sports/, the *Dallas Morning News* newspaper

LONGHORNS ADORE AUSTIN

Austin, Texas, not only has the extreme good luck to be the home city of the beautiful University of Texas at Austin campus, it's also the capital city of the great state of Texas.

The self-proclaimed "Live Music Capital of the World," Austin is home to both the famous South by Southwest music festival